Love
Misinterpreted

JAMES RUSSELL ROUNDTREE

ISBN 979-8-88751-341-6 (paperback)
ISBN 979-8-88751-342-3 (digital)

Christian Faith Publishing
832 Park Avenue
Meadville, PA 16335
www.christianfaithpublishing.com

Printed in the United States of America

Introduction

M y mother and grandmother inspired me to write this book. My grandmother is deceased, and my mother is ninety-one, still living today. My oldest daughter, Helki Roundtree, helped me edit my work. My daughter Asia Roundtree inspired me to write this book based on my struggles and failures in life. I dedicate this memory to my father Fred that passed away, complicated man in my life.

I have witnessed many failed relationships in my family. My parents were born in the South. My father and mother married in North Carolina. In my early years, I was raised in Norfolk, Virginia. I missed those early years. My mother moved my brothers and me to Connecticut. I was about the age of eleven. I witnessed my own failed relationships, two marriages. I was already set up to fail in a relationship. My father was not a true example of a husband and father. I never saw any true value in the man, although I love him. Mother and Father divorced by the time I was six years old. I was blessed not to have him living in same house. I will explain it as I write each chapter.

All the men in my life were bad examples to me. It took me years to figure out how to love. Later, I will go in deep how I developed true love for my third wife. Why am I writing this book? Many couples fail to understand the true meaning of love. Many relationships are doomed before it starts. Most people do not understand love. Lust has a lot to do with it but not love. Why did I fail to deal with family members that tried to molest my daughters? Why did I fail to take a DNA test? These are mistakes I made as a young man that I often think about in my old age, situations where I could have made life less complicated for my daughters if I was not so busy working all the time. I thought I was making the right decision at that time. How can we ease the pain of our beloved children when attacked by family? I will share my pain as a father and husband from life experiences. We can be better mates if we take time to listen to the other person instead of self.

We should understand our family history, our forefathers before us. This will help us understand why other family members abuse other family members. Generation curses are passed down to the next generation. Why do members of the family lack love? Love of God has not truly been passed down to the next generation. How can we understand ourselves if we cannot understand our past? This will tell us why we behave a certain way. I wanted to understand why I practiced fornication and adultery. This seemed to be normal behavior growing up. No one took the time to explain why people cannot fully love, a violation of God's principles. Time is something you cannot get back, and love can be lost.

The young should understand love. I did not quite understand it. Many young people confuse love with sex, that is why so many are lost. It took me years to understand love. I was never taught by my father how to love because he never knew how to love. I found true love through Christ. The Bible is a true inspiration for love. I learned to love my woman. I will explain why my first marriage was set up for failure, and my second marriage had no chance to survive, the pain of becoming a man at eighteen years old venturing into unknown territory. I am writing this book for my children and grandchildren to know the importance of love in any relationship. There is nothing wrong with showing affection to your wife and children. It keeps the bond of love together. It is much needed in the family. Family structure is important. Embracing your wife with a kiss and touching keeps you grounded, and so does embracing your children with the same love.

Chapter 1

My grandfather Turner married Doris and later were divorced, leaving him to be a single parent. My grandfather remarried his second wife Melinda. I was attached to my daughters. I inherited that nature from my grandfather, Turner. He was short and bow legged. My brother and I stayed with him and my step-grandmother when we visited him in the country. During those days, outdoor toilets were popular. We chased the chicken around the yard. We listened to crickets at night. My grandfather was the only man I thought had true love between a man and a woman.

When I was thirteen years old, I always wanted to be a good father. I had no idea what a good husband was supposed to be at that time. My father was not a good example as a husband. He often cheated on my mother. He had a few children outside of marriage during their marriage. I did not know too much about what kind of work he did as a living, but he did work. One day, my father and mother took me downtown to shop for clothes. We caught the bus back home and my father punched my mother in the nose and she was crying walking me home. I did not like it, but I was a child in a helpless situation. As a child, I was contemplating in my mind; I would have protected my mother from his abuse. I suffered for many years from that situation. I never wanted to be like him.

I had fun times living on Legion Street. My neighbors were down-to-earth people. Mickey's mother did not cook homemade biscuits, so he came to my house with his brother. I sold him the biscuit with syrup. Mickey's family grew their vegetables and fruits. All the neighborhood children would go out at night to steal their

1

fruits. They grew sweet strawberries, apples, and pears. Gary was the preacher's son. I felt sorry for him. He had to do all the chores for his sisters. He had to wash clothes by hand. During that time period, his baby sister messed up in those diapers. Gary could not stay out late like us; his grandmother would yell out loud that it was time to come in the house. Bernie was another friend who had to go in their house early; a minute late, and he got beaten. Johnny was our leader. Everybody looked up to him. He was my best friend. He loves all kinds of sports. Johnny had all good-looking sisters. My childhood was fun. I remembered one day, Johnny and I walked across a bridge to go to a movie. I was barefoot, and the pavement was hot. We never did go see that movie. I will never walk barefoot again. We did some crazy things too, for example, sliding down a steep hill on cardboard boxes. I cut my leg. I have that scar on my leg today.

My mother and father had six children. My sister is the only girl. My father had four outside children, and it could be more. I knew some of them during my childhood and met my half-sister in my late twenties. My father never knew about true love. His mother died when he was three, and my grandmother refused to let him live with his father. He grew up with his older uncles. He was never taught to respect a woman. He never fully loved my mother. He never taught his sons and daughters to respect their relationship. But he had some clues about marriage. Both my grandmother's husbands were preachers, but my father was driven by lust. My older brothers were driven by the same lustful spirits as well as the rest of his children.

My mother remarried when I was about eight. I met my stepfather for the first time when she brought him home. "This is your new stepfather," she said. My stepfather brought his six children. There were nine children in a three-bedroom house. Oatmeal was the main breakfast every morning. My stepfather was not a true example as a role model. He stayed drunk and would go to work. My mother moved me and my brothers to live in Connecticut. I hated moving to Connecticut, leaving all my childhood friends. I cried many nights. My grandmother comforted me that things will get better. My grandmother raised my sister. That is the main reason I am not connected to my sister. I should have been raised with my sister. We are one year apart.

My older brothers started making babies at fifteen, and my mother left them to live in the same house. Both my brothers were married by seventeen. They knew nothing about love; no father figure. They were never taught to respect a woman. They repeated the same sin of my father's. Fornication was in their makeup. My brothers acted upon what they saw in my father's children out of wedlock. I had no role models. I was about twelve years old when all this unfaithfulness took place. My sisters-in-law were faithful wives. My oldest brother, Sam, never physically abused his wife, only spiritually and mentally. Next to the oldest is my brother, Ralph, also an abuser mentally and spiritually. They were not perfect examples of role-model husbands. Rebecca would have been a good example as a husband, but she is a woman. She could not hold on to a husband because her husband was just like her brothers. They were driven by the lust of the flesh. True love is as strong as death. Cruelty will drive a man to his grave. These men wrecked their marriages, having no regrets. They bragged about their mistresses. None of them tried to keep the family together; they cherished evil. The men had no respect for themselves or the wife they were hurting. All their evil deeds work against them. Those bastard children were still left without a father. The children lost out because no fathers were in either homes. Sam's and Ralph's wives left them to start life over again—all these children growing up without a father in the home. Most of these children will grow up with lack of respect in their relationships. They will repeat the sins of their fathers. Most of them will not know the true value of a relationship unless they are taught the true value of marriage. Fornication is not God's plan but to abstain from sex until marriage. Children must be taught early to value their bodies. We must teach them about predators.

I remember when I was about six. The babysitter showed me her private parts and had me get on top of her. Somewhere in her life, she was not taught about exposing her body. I was too young to understand what she was doing to me. My father was never around to teach me the danger of people taking advantage of me. My mother worked all the time to provide for me. My oldest brothers were not old enough themselves to explain sex to me.

My mother took me and my youngest to visit my father in jail. I never knew what crime he did. I was too young. He was absent from the home. My father was no spiritual leader even though he knew the Bible.

Life was great in Virginia. The neighborhood children always went to Johnny's mother's house to eat. His mother always had plenty of hot dogs to go around. Mothers look out for each other's welfare. That is the main reason I hated moving to Connecticut to live. All my friends' families were closely knitted. I did go back to live at thirteen with Sam for a year. I reconnected with my childhood friends in junior high school. There was a big difference in how you were disciplined in school. In Connecticut, you were not allowed to beat the children, but in Virginia, you could beat the children. I went to Campostella Junior High School. John and I were caught running in the cafeteria. Our gym teacher caught us and had us come to the gym. The gym teacher had us bent over and hit us hard with a thick paddle. I never got in trouble anymore.

I had only one fight outside of school. All the neighborhood boys went to play basketball, and this older boy, eighteen, tried to bully me, and I was not going to be bullied, so he punched me in the eye. I was caught off guard. I went on to tell my brother Sam about the encounter. So my brother Sam had me fight him the next week. Neither one of us was wrong. After the fight, I was exhausted. I did not go to school that day. I went home and fell asleep from the fight. I never saw Bill again. We all are faced with bullies at one point in our lives.

I want the reader to understand that generation curses can be broken. Once you understand where your generation curse originated from, you can seek guidance to solve it in your life. Most people do not try to understand why they act a certain way. You must understand the previous generations' curses. Lying could be your family generation curse or overuse of alcohol, maybe stealing from other people. It could be a combination of all curses. Once you recognize your generation curses, things can change if you pray on being delivered.

Sam and Ralph never learned from our father's generation curse going from woman to woman. I took notes from my father's and brothers' infidelity. I observed for years their noncommitment to those women. I thought their behavior was normal. I practiced fornication until I got married. None of these men taught me correct behavior. They glorified their behavior. Most boys are not taught to be men by their fathers even if they are around them. Some boys have no fathers at all. It is hard for mothers to teach their sons love regarding a girl if they have not been given it by a man. Women beaten down by disrespect from their spouses find it hard to train their sons on love when they have not received it themselves. Most mothers see their sons as like their fathers. My mother could not teach my brothers true love for a woman because she never received true love from her husband. She knew his mistress and their babies. My father did not love himself. I asked him that question about love. Did he really love anyone? He could not answer the question. He never knew the meaning of love. If he did, why did he keep hurting my mother with his lustful spirit? True love is when you protect the other person's feelings, something he never taught his children. My father never protected my mother's heart. My mother never taught me how to respect a young heart. I became my father and my brothers.

My mother's heart was broken so many times. She tried her best to raise five sons with an absentee husband. She taught us the basic things on how to survive. We had to do womanly duties, for example, to wash clothes, wash the dishes, and make our bed. We were well disciplined, and she made sure we went to church. When she went to work, the neighbor took us to church. I remember going to a Baptist church in Norfolk, Virginia. We were taught to stay still on the pews or chairs. Mothers stuck together. There's no place like home, meaning Virginia. I remember I took some candy out of the store, and my mother gave it to the owner to return it. I was spanked with a switch. I never did it again.

Life changed for me when I moved to Stamford, Connecticut. My mother's skin is white as snow, and her beauty is like Queen Sheba, but it came with a cost, the cost of not being Black enough in a White body. In school, I was always bullied. She had to fight her way in school. My father is pure Black and handsome. He was not over five feet and four inches tall. My mother struggled in school because of her color and natural beauty.

I never saw color until I moved to Stamford, Connecticut, to our new apartment on 17 Woodland Avenue. It was a six-family house. I lived on the first floor. On the third was a boy named Ron. One day, I was in the backyard minding my business. He called my mother White, and I responded back by calling his mother Black. She was black as tar and fat. He was Black like his mother, not so fair looking. I was a handsome boy. This is the first time I experienced racism in my race. He continued to bully me, so we always were fighting. I never liked fighting. My mother taught us to avoid trouble. She taught us Christian values. I was eleven when he started to bully me, and it continued on to junior high school. I got the best of him at last. Ron won many battles, but I won the war. I never liked him after all those encounters. I hated fighting, but there were moments I had to defend myself. My father demonstrated enough violence in my early years.

I was shy for years. I adjusted to my new environment. I met new friends, Tom and Dick. Dick lived on the second floor, and Tom lived around the corner. Tom was my first friend in elementary. He was a bad boy. He got into fights all the time on the bus. Vanessa and Tom fought often. Vanessa was like a tomboy, rough on the edges. She was not afraid of us. I only got into one fight with her. She gave me a black eye. Tom had a racetrack. My mother bought me a racetrack. Tom came over a lot to race his cars. We got into fights often, and he tried to switch bodies. We remained friends. Tom taught me how to make money. He took me to the train station and showed me the ropes to shine shoes. I made more money than him shining shoes. I went all the time, later exposing myself to stealing. I went to stores to steal cars for our racetrack. I stole more than him. I always outdid him. By the time we got to junior high, he taught me how to steal clothes. I went with him, and security saw us put clothes under our shirt. The security guard chased us around the store. Tom ran out the building because he knew his surroundings. I ran upstairs and was caught by security. The store manager called the police, and I was taken to the police station. The police never booked me. He called my mother. My mother picked me up in her Delta 88. She had two adult men to hold me down. She beat me so hard with an extension cord. I never stole again. I stopped being around Tom. He was not a good influence for me. Tom never stopped stealing. By the time he got to high school, he was stealing cars. We did some crazy things as children. We made our go-carts with wheels and went down steep hills onto the street. We could have been driven over by a car. I looked back; that was dangerous.

Dick moved into the building when I started junior high. We all went to Dolan Junior High. Dick and I were friends for a short period. He lived on the second floor. We had some fights over small things. Once I started high school, I never saw too much of him. He started hanging around bad teenagers. They stayed out late all night. Their mothers did not care that much. They came home anytime. Dick and Rob had no specific time to be at home, but my mother had a set time. If we were not home on time, my brothers and I were punished. He did not go to school like me. We played basketball and football together. Dick and his new friends like robbing people and beating up White people. I was not raised that way, so I avoided contact with his crew. Dick looked up to Rob, his new friend. He looked up to Rob like a god. Whatever Rob did, he did as well. They stayed out all night. School did not matter to them. We all played pool together, but I knew when to go home. Rob was the leader of the group, and whatever he did, the rest followed. I went to the corner store to play pool on the tables, but Jeff was the best pool shooter. They gambled sometimes on the pool table. I never gambled with them, only as a spectator. It did not make sense for me to gamble. I could not beat anyone in the group. We played cards for money I had no problem winning at times. I once saw a policeman kill a man on the third floor.

Rob and Jeff started robbing liquor stores with another man. The man in the liquor store was shot by Jake. They were arrested and went to jail. Rob and Jake did eight years, and Jeff did five years. Jeff's mother knew people in high places, and his cousin was a policeman.

The word in the neighborhood was Jeff gave up information to a lesser sentence. Most of them had no fathers living with them, nor did they have any contact with their fathers. Only five of us actually had our fathers around us, and out of the five, two were faithful to their wives.

Rock's father was a family man who encouraged his children to attain a higher education. I never heard anything negative about Rock's father. Rock and his sister graduated and went to college. All the other young men got a job after graduation. My parents never talked about college to us. Jake's father stayed drunk all the time. He had no control over Jake. Jake stayed in trouble throughout his life. We had some fun times together. Hank's father stayed at the bar all the time, but Hank never got in any trouble even though his father was making children outside of his marriage to his wife. He was a quiet man. Jake and I became best friends in high school and still are friends today. We played basketball all the time at the community center and had parties.

None of my friends knew how to treat a girl or girlfriend. They knew nothing about respecting a young girl. Most of them came from broken homes that were never taught love. They were never faithful to a woman. They had multiple girlfriends. Rob had babies by two different girls. He took turns sleeping at each other's houses. He was supported by the ladies. They cooked his meals and washed his clothes like a king. They gave him money when he needed it. Jack was the only person who stayed with his childhood sweetheart and married her after high school. Jack's only problem was drugs. He loved using dope and smoking angel dust and other drugs. All the guys in the neighborhood did drugs except me. Most of them smoked cigarettes. I tried a puff and did not like it. It was a bad feeling, and I never tried it again. Jake had multiple girlfriends but was the complete opposite of Rob; Jake had his girlfriends get abortions. He had no conscience destroying life. His father stayed drunk all the time to teach him respect. Jake never knew love.

The basement of 17 Woodland Avenue is where we formed our club. We named the club Five Centage, and Ralph was the leader. He was the bigger and stronger of the group. There were other clubs on each side of town. There was only one fight among the clubs, and no one got hurt. We used our hands, and weapons were not involved at all. The next week, we were playing basketball again. South End and Village were friends, and other clubs did not want to fight. The Village had a reputation for fighting. Juice was the Village leader, and his whole family was feared. The Village guys were going with the girls in our neighborhood, and we became acquainted with them. The South End became stronger with their support. We never had any problems with any other. We fought against the West Side and won the battle. George fought their number one man, Rick. Both of them were well built. George, our man, won.

When I entered high school, girls were all over the place liking me. My first girlfriend was Emma. Emma was the sweetest girl I ever knew in my life. Emma's mother and father were kind people. I almost had sex with her in my basement, but my mother prevented it. She told us to come upstairs, and I never tried it again with Emma.

My first year of high school, nine other girls became my interests after Emma. Michelle and Pamsy started liking me; no sex. I started liking Sally and forgot about the other girls. Renita and I had sex one time but had no real relationship. It was over. I never engaged in sex again with her. By the time I got to tenth grade, more girls started liking me. This girl in the eleventh grade started liking me when she was in my algebra class. She gave me her telephone number and address. I went to her house a few times, but nothing happened. I stopped going to see her. I was never a person to force myself on any girl.

After school was out for the summer, I never thought about girls that much. I was too busy working. I was trying to save money for my school clothes. When I went back to school in the fall, some other girls started liking me. Now I was in the eleventh grade. I met my high school girlfriend that year. She spoke a little English. She was my main girlfriend. I was not trying to have sex with her because she was a Christian. So I was having sex with other girls. I respected her over the other girls. Judy started liking me. She was an easy prey. She came over to my house, and we had sex for hours. After she left, I never saw her again.

I was not trying to have sex with my girlfriend. I never thought of myself fornicating back then. I knew little about the Bible and its understanding. My girlfriend's people were from Costa Rica. She had five sisters and two brothers. Brook's mother was a kind and gentle person. Whenever I walked to the East Side to see my girlfriend, her mother gave me a ride back to South End. Her stepfather got me a dish washing job at a golf club. I worked there all summer. It opened up doors for a better job. When I went back to school. I bought all my school clothes. I ate a few times at her mother's house. I loved the salad that was prepared and the rice. They made their own salad dressing. My mother never made salad; it was different. It was delicious. I never took time to learn their native language, Spanish. Gregory Street was the place to go. I remember her mother's blue Volkswagen. I drove it one time. I cared about her but had no clue on how to respect her. I was never taught the true meaning of love and respect. I never had a solid role model.

My girlfriend's stepfather was not a perfect example of a husband. He was cheating on his wife every weekend. Mrs. Jackie dropped him to the train station every Friday and picked him up every Sunday night from the train station. He did not love her. He was living with her for his children. He never loved his stepdaughter. They argued a lot over that situation. Mrs. Jackie had to be mother and father to my girlfriend. Some of her sisters were jealous of her because of her skin color, and they felt she looked better. They all were beautiful, well-built girls, but my girlfriend was excellent in beauty. Maria, the oldest, was kind and generous like her mother. She always respected me for some reason. She was always there for me. She will always be in my heart. Sally, the next-to-oldest sister, never cared for me for some reasons, was not kind and generous. The rest were normal.

In my last year of high school, I only had two classes to take and work study. The school found me a job at a shoe store. I had five girls liking me that year. I had sex with some of them. I caught venereal disease that year. That was the only time in my life I caught a sexual disease. This was the year I started having sex with my girlfriend. She finally gave it to me. She was a virgin, and she was not happy losing her virginity. She cried about it and said she was going to tell her stepfather, but she never did. We continued having sex. We never used any protection. She was trying to teach me the Bible. It did a lot of good, and my grades got better. I made the honor roll for two years.

I never did drugs until the last year. I started to get lost. I let my guard down. I started hanging out with Buster and George. I started drinking and going to parties. Buster was in one of my classes. The girls went crazy over him. He loved being around White boys. So one day, I went to his house, and he gave me half a pill to swallow. It did nothing to me. I did not know what I was getting myself into at that time. He gave me the other half, and I flipped out. It was acidic. I got paranoid and ran out of his house to my side of town. It was twenty minutes away. I got to the telephone and called my girlfriend's oldest sister. Maria came to the South End and took me back to their house. I stayed all night until the drugs wore off. All I could see that night was the ceiling turning around with stars. I vomited black stuff that night. I never did LSD again. I had setbacks for a whole week. I said Psalm 23 every day until I was back to normal. I almost got run over by a trunk that night.

I continued learning about the Bible, but I still was dealing with the lust of the flesh from my surroundings. The only conceivable sin is the flesh, overcoming my sexual appetite. One puff of cigarette, and it was over. After that encounter, I never had Buster as a friend. I continued seeing my girlfriend, and her family never talked to me about if I was still doing drugs. I began to focus on getting better grades. I did have some discussion about going to college and marriage one day. Dot never did drugs or drink alcohol. She was too much into the Bible. That is what made her special over the other girls. If she never would have had sex, I would not have pressured her. I always tell Christian girls and boys to stick with someone who believed what they believed. Do not waste your time to convert anyone you put yourself at risk. If I knew the true meaning of love, I would not have had sex with any of those girls. I would have waited for the right time for marriage and not engaged in fornication. My father never had any conversation about marriage or sex. I was on my own.

On my way to graduate from high school, I got the bad news from my girlfriend that she was pregnant. I remembered having sex with her behind the wall at the shoe store and sometimes at my house. My mother moved back to Virginia to her second husband. My mother wanted me and my brothers to move back home, but I did not have any good reason to go back home. I was graduating in six months from Stamford High. I worked at a Holland shoe store. I was in a work study program after school. I was earning my own money but was not expecting to be a father. So I had to break the bad news to my guidance counselor that I will not be going to college. I was not up to it, but I had to engage in a conversation with her regarding my education. I was looking forward to going to college. That was one of my dreams besides being an entrepreneur.

I had an appointment to meet with Mrs. Salmon to discuss my girlfriend's pregnancy. I told her I could not go to college because I was expecting a baby in November that school year. Mrs. Salmon suggested I could live on campus with my girlfriend. I did not think it was a good idea, so I told her I would get a job. Marriage was not mine. It was suggested by her mother. They were embarrassed about her getting pregnant, and they told her to ask me to marry her, so I agreed with them. They first wanted us to get an abortion. I was not for any abortion because my mother taught me to be a responsible person. If I got anyone pregnant, I'd be man enough to take care of my baby. I decided to marry her after graduation.

In June 1974, we engaged in matrimony. I got a job at Poly Cast being a glass operator making glass windows at night. The company shipped glass windows for building. For six months, we lived in her mother's house. My wife and I got baptized at the Seventh-Day Adventist Church. We were taught the Scriptures. We loved going to church every Sabbath, but I was not fully connected to God. But she was connected. She prayed a lot, but I didn't pray at all. I didn't quite understand prayer and how it works.

We finally moved into our first apartment. I was tempted by this married lady. I fell into the devil's trap, lust of the flesh. One night when my wife was asleep, I pursued the married woman. I went to her house a few times to engage in sex, but nothing happened. I stopped going to her house. I never had sex with her. I had no idea what I was doing to myself, being driven by the curse of lust my father left me, being unfaithful. My father could not teach me how to respect my marriage; he never respected my mother. He cared about her but never knew the true meaning of love. If you really love the person, you stay faithful. I cared about my wife, but I did not know the true meaning of love. When you love a person, you do not hurt them emotionally.

Later, we moved into a rent-controlled apartment across town. We lived on the seventeenth floor. We continued to go to church every week. We did have our firstborn when living at her mother's house. We were expecting the baby in November, on my birthday. My wife's water broke on my birthday. We rushed her to Stamford Hospital. She finally had a baby girl. She was so pretty and cute. We gave her an Indian name from a book with names. It was not a common name you give a Black child. It means "to touch." I never thought about being with any woman but my wife.

I always did the laundry at home. So one day, I went downstairs to do the laundry, and trouble came my way. This young woman came up to me and said she would grab my penis. I never heard this kind of talk from a woman. I thought she was playing. She actually did it. I did not know too much about the behavior of females. So I lost control. I lusted after her, and I got involved sexually. I started going to bars and gambling places. I took her to the beach one time and had sex with her, and the police almost caught us. It would have been embarrassing if I was arrested. My wife's mother would have been disappointed in me, especially spending money on a big wedding. This was the last time going to the park with her. The woman paid for a hotel for us. We had sex again. I never enjoyed sex with her; just got caught up in some mess. I cared about her in that way. I had no feelings for her, just sex. I never spent money on her. In the end, I told her I was finished with her. During that time, I was having another baby with my wife. I knew my wife was unhappy because I was hanging out too much. I decided to move us out of the building. So I moved us across town to save my marriage. I never looked back. I made a big mistake. I stayed faithful to her, my wife.

I found a new job at Clairol, a manufacturer of hair products. My job was making hair products. I loved it. The money was good for someone coming out of high school. My first car was a 1969 Chevy Malibu my sister cosigned for me. It was yellow. I bought it after I got married. My second car, two years later, was a Ford Torino, sky blue. My second daughter was born the next year, 1977. I was focused on church and work.

My wife finished high school after our first daughter was born. I made sure she finished her education. We talked about getting more education by the time we moved into a housing authority. My wife never worked during the marriage, and she wanted to go to design school in New York City. So we agreed that she would go back to school first, then I would go after she finished. She did graduate, and she was good at it. I did not go back to school while we were living together, only after the separation. She did get me involved in business.

I bought a distributorship from ISIS Industries. My wife told me about the company. That is how I got involved with business. It did not work out, but I learned about business. I went door-to-door to the beauty salons. I did sell the products but failed to show customers how to use them. So the business flopped, but I never gave up on business.

After she graduated from school, she landed her first job as a designer in Stamford, Connecticut. This is when her love affair started, at her job in 1979. She always talked about these guys at her job, but I never thought she was cheating. I took it as a casual conversation. One night, she never came home. I knew something was wrong, but I did not think she was having an affair. I called her best friend. I had no idea what was happening, so I called her mother. Her mother knew nothing and had no clue. I was in the dark for the first time. It never crossed my mind that she was having a love affair. I always had been the only person she had ever been sexually involved with throughout the years. My heart led me to her coworker's house. So I decided to go to Franklin Street. She always talked about them. She gave me the address in a previous conversation. So I went there the next morning to Franklin Street, and his friend said she went down to his friend's house. I knocked on his friend's door, and they came to the door together. She claimed she did nothing but fell asleep. I did not believe her. I was so mad I beat her with a belt. I was never a wife beater. I was against hitting any woman. I lost control of myself. I never put a hand on her again.

She continued to see him while living with me. I lost my feelings for her. She contracted a venereal disease from him, but I never caught anything. I stopped having sex with her. My love for her dropped. I was badly hurt. She continued seeing him while still living with me. She claimed it was only work related, not physical contact. This was the first time she was attracted to another man. I lost my edge in the relationship. I never trusted her after her involvement with another man. We had two beautiful daughters during this time. I tried getting her involved back with the church, but she lost hope. I tried to forgive her, but the pain was there.

She was never a woman to go to parties but her oldest sister's parties. I never knew her to drink any type of liquor or do drugs. So one night, she went to a party with her sisters, and I knew nothing about it. This was another occasion when she disappeared on me. I called her family house, and her stepfather answered the phone. He gave me the address to the party. I was drinking that night. It was in Brooklyn, New York. I did not know too much about the place, but somehow, I found it. I was down and out, very depressed. I found the party and went inside the apartment. She was there with her three sisters. I went up to my wife and asked her to come home. She did not resist me. We started walking toward my car, and she got into the car, but her sister tried to pull her out of the car. I told her sister she was coming home with me and her sister grabbed me and we got into a fight. I was not trying to get into a physical fight; it just happened. My wife and I went back to Connecticut. The next day, I was not happy about getting into the fight. I tried apologizing, but no one wanted to accept my apology. Her brother came over to fight, but nothing happened. He left my house and never came back. If he would have broken my door, I was going to cut him. I showed him the knife. I was from the hood, and I was going to protect myself.

My wife started working with her lover in my house. I did not care at that moment that my feelings were not there. I stopped them from working in my house. It wasn't right having her lover at my house. I was still going to church. I never expected her to commit adultery when she got me involved with God and the church. I did seek counseling from my pastor. She was not interested in saving the marriage, so I finally gave up on the marriage temporarily. I gave the apartment up, and she moved back with her mother. She continued seeing her lover. I got involved in her designing, and I started giving professional fashion shows to get her exposed to the world. I put together a group of girls to model her clothes. My wife was in the show. I invested a lot of time and money getting her name out there. I was not focused on the marriage anymore. I lost interest in her. I continued to work and see my daughters. I was living back in my old neighborhood again. I was living with my sister. I was separated from my wife and children for the first time. After the fashion show, everything fell apart. I was heartbroken when the fashion show was not a success. I actually cried when it was over. At that point, we got farther apart. I moved to my sister's house. I was still friends with my wife's cousin. I went over to his house a lot to play on his pool table. He would inform me about everything she was doing in her life. The bad news he gave me at his house was that she took my children with her new lover to California. I cried the second time in my life; my children were not here. My wife's family was not going to tell me where she went with my children. I thought I would never see them again. I continued to work and focus on myself. My sister had a long talk with me about overcoming her.

Weeks and months went by, and no word from her. I missed my daughters. This was the first time I felt something was missing from my family. I worked as a security guard at my brother-in-law's job, and he must have given her my telephone. I moved out of my sister's house into my friend's grandmother's apartment. My wife finally gave me a call on my job. She stated her lover left her, and she needed help with the children. She wanted us to get back together and repair the marriage. So I decided to move to Long Beach, California. I saved up $7,000 and got my plane tickets. My landlord told me I was taking a risk. I should not go there because bad things sometimes happen. I did not worry about anything bad happening to me. I trusted in God; I would be protected. I told Ms. Nancy I was buying a plane ticket to California, and I did purchase my ticket the next week. I was happy that I was getting back with my family. I did not think about her ex-boyfriend once I got there.

Once I landed in California, I went to the nearest car dealer and bought a Gremlin. It was a small car. Then I called her to let her know I was there. She gave me the address before I came out there. When I arrived at her house, I knocked on her door. She came to the door and opened it. I went inside her apartment. There was no furniture in the house except a queen-sized mattress in her bedroom. The apartment smelled like vomit, not fresh, and there was no food in the refrigerator. My children were not accustomed to those bad conditions; they always had a bed to sleep on and food to eat. I guessed she was depending on the welfare check her mother was supposed to send her from Connecticut along with the welfare check she would get in California. She was banking on two checks from two different states, but I messed up her plan by contacting the Connecticut Welfare Department. When her cousin told me she moved to California, I went to her mother's house and looked in the mailbox, and there was the state check. I reported welfare fraud, and the state discontinued the check. This did not give her enough time to get off the ground. She could not handle the responsibility herself because I always paid the bills. So she decided to call me to rescue her. I took her and my children grocery shopping. I bought enough food to last for a few weeks. Then we went back to her apartment. She helped me bring the food inside the apartment. The refrigerator was full of food. So I bought a car and food the day I arrived.

She put the food in the refrigerator while we were talking to each other, then I heard the key opening up the door. It was her lover who was shocked to see me there. She was lying to both of us. He came straight to the kitchen and went to the kitchen sink and grabbed a long knife. He was coming straight toward me to cut me. She grabbed the knife from him. We fought from the front room to the back room, and she panicked. My wife called the police while we were fighting. We wrestled each other, but no one threw any punches. Next thing, the police came to the door, and we stopped fighting. We came to the front, and the police asked her what happened. She told the police we were fighting, and the police wanted to know who we were. She told the police she did not know her lover, and I was her husband. She lied to the police, and her lover told the officers he moved her to California from Connecticut. They were living together, and he did not know why I was there. I told the officers she told me that she broke up with her lover. She wanted to get back together. The officers told her they locked people up for lying, so they asked both of us to leave her apartment. Now I knew what Ms. Nancy was talking about. Sometimes people do not make it. He was going to stab me, but God was with me. It was time for me to come back to Connecticut.

I went back to my hotel and went back to her house the next morning. I had made plans to take my daughters back to Connecticut. So I went back to my wife's apartment to see my children again. I knocked on her door, and she said come inside. I went straight to her bedroom. She was lying down on the mattress on the floor with her lover and my daughters. I told her I wanted no trouble, just wanted to take my daughters back to the hotel to spend some time with them. She let me take my daughters, and I went straight to the car dealer to sell the car back. I told the dealer I had no plans staying in California. I needed my money back. The dealer gave me all the money except the taxes. God was with me. I took a cab to the airport and bought three tickets. The children were too young to understand what was taking place. The children were only three and six. It was summertime, and I was out there one day. It was getting hot out there, and I am not talking about body heat but evil. We arrived at the airport and went to the counter to buy my tickets. We left at night. Before boarding the plane, I gave her a phone call that I was boarding a plane with my daughters, and they were never coming to California anymore. I never called her anymore. We landed in Connecticut the next morning. I went to live with my sister. We stayed in the room together until I got on my feet. I found a job.

She stayed in California for a few months before coming back to Connecticut. She did come back but not for the children, just to bring dirty clothes I had to wash. I was happy having my daughters back home. My daughters never went to California anymore. Things went bad with her and her lover. She returned back to California to be with her boyfriend. She stayed out there another six months before returning back home to Connecticut. He sold her expensive sewing machine and left her. Their relationship ended, and she moved back with her mother. So I talked to her about getting an apartment to raise the children, but her mother did not like that idea. Mother told me, "I would do everything in my power to keep you both from getting back together." We never got back together, and the children went back and forth between us both. At that point, she was only concerned about her career. Since I did not see any future of getting back together, I started dating this girl. We were living separate lives. I only focused on my daughters.

Chapter 2

Dawn was a nice young lady who finished college. She was Jamaican. She was very refined. Dawn went to the movies with me and my daughters to see *The Color Purple*. It was a good movie. Dawn's mother likes me a lot. I visited them at their apartment. We dated for months, but we never engaged in sex. We were getting to know each other's personalities. She was a respectable young lady. Even though we were separated, my wife had a way of getting back into my life. She found out about Dawn, and now she wanted us to get back together. I fell for it. I allowed her to talk me back into being together as a family. So we engaged in sex again, thinking she wanted us to be married, as husband and wife. I broke up with Dawn to put the family back together. After I broke up with Dawn, my wife left town again. Now I had broken Dawn's heart. She really liked me. I could not get my wife out of my system. She had a hold on me. She did not want me to be with anyone. After I moved into a room with my daughters, the lady next door would babysit the girls when I went back to work. Their mother left town again for months.

I never thought I would be single raising children, but I love my daughters. They came first in my life. I spent time with them. I took them to the parks on occasion. I spent time teaching them how to read. I enjoyed being a father. Later, I met a Spanish girl and went out with her. I never had sex with her. I took her to my brother's house to meet my family. Then my wife came back to town, and we started talking again. She acted like she wanted to get back to me, so I stopped talking to that girl. I only knew her for a week, so there was no hard feelings between the both of us. My wife left again, to New

Jersey. I still had not figured it out yet. She never wanted to get back. She just did not want anyone to have me. She was a bitter and angry woman. I stayed focused on my daughter. The last time she came back, she filed for divorced. She wanted me to sign my daughters to the state, but I disagreed. She sold herself to the devil. She lost her Christian values. She was the person that turned me to God and read the Scriptures. She turned me into prayer, now she is living a worldly life, jumping from man to man, putting those things before her children. She once told me when dating her lover she would never be good to me. She was right; no interest in marriage. She jumped into an unknown world when she broke her wedding vows. She got involved with a worldly man. He turned her out. This was the second man she ever had sex; I always been the only one. She could never love me. She was exposed to another world she was not prepared for. She left God and the church, something she was accustomed to. The spirit of evil entered her soul. She left town again, and I met Tammy.

I was walking to the club, and I met Tammy. I knew her from my friend Tommy. We were not close friends. I knew him from grow- ing up. Tommy was Tammy's boyfriend, but they broke up. Tammy gave me a ride to work one time. We both worked in Greenwich, Connecticut. I was walking on the other side of town back home when Tammy was walking to her father's house. I was leaving my sister's place. She broke up with her boyfriend. Somehow, we started talking to each other and became good friends. I was living in the same room. So we started going together. I had no car. I was saving up for a car. Then I finally bought myself a car. My oldest brother took me to New York to buy a car. I bought a Cutlass Supreme, a pretty white car with maroon velvet seat covers.

My wife came back to town again. The children were back at her mother's house again. This time, she did not come back to break us up but to finalize the divorce. After I moved out of my room into my girlfriend's father's house. She decided to move back to New Jersey again without the children. The children were at her mother's house again. So me and my new girlfriend were getting along well. We both had jobs. Next thing, my soon-to-be ex-wife dropped the children at her house and told her grandmother she was going to New Jersey, and I can have the children. In the process, her grandmother saw her break the car windows of my new car.

Most of my friends were going to the prom when I was getting married. In June 1974, I was a married man expecting a baby in November 1974. I was home when my wife was getting labor pains, and soon, her water broke. The contractions were getting closer and closer by the hour. I was excited about the baby coming on my birthday. My wife's water finally broke, and her oldest sister rushed us to the hospital. She was admitted to hospital. I waited outside the room until the doctor came to deliver the baby. I went inside the room to watch the baby being born. We had a baby girl. We gave her an Indian name we chose from a name book. My baby daughter was so beautiful. During those days, the woman stayed in the hospital for at least three days.

I found my first job at this glass company making glass. I worked the night shift. It was not a hard job. I worked for about six months to save money for an apartment. I started looking for an apartment to move out of her mother's house. Weeks later, I found an apartment near the village, the projects for low income. It was a two-bedroom apartment. We lived there for about two years. I was the only one working while she completed her high school education. We were doing well. We went to church every Sabbath. We both studied under the new pastor. We were thoroughly taught the Scriptures. Life was moving along in the right direction.

I was still plagued with my father's nature—lust. This girl I knew from the past invited me to her house. I was tricked by my father, the devil, and went over there. One night when my wife was asleep, I went to her house. I never did anything with her. I went a few times. I was not comfortable with the situation because she was a married woman. My conscience would not allow me to follow through with evil. She was a very attractive woman. I was only twenty at that time, but I knew it was wrong. I walked away from her and never saw her anymore.

I was a newborn Christian but weak spiritually. I didn't quite understand prayer like my wife. I still had some heathen ways. I wanted to be a Christian but did not know how to be one. We continued to go to church Sabbath after Sabbath. But there was a temptation in the church. My wife's cousin, a young woman, was trying to feel my penis under the table. We all sat close together. I never told my wife about her cousin trying to feel my penis. I did not like what she was doing to me in church. I never thought things like that would happen in church. Sue was completely out of line. I never confronted her about her behavior. I learned later she got pregnant and was smoking those funny cigarettes with her boyfriend. I was too young to understand females lust just like men. I knew the scriptures but did not know how to apply it to my life, but I could feel when something was wrong. I was still growing as a Christian.

I never spent time with my siblings. I was too busy working. I went back to my old neighborhood to play basketball but did not go a lot. One of my childhood friends got an attitude while playing basketball. He was too aggressive to me, and he wanted to fight. I put away childish things. I had a wife and two daughters to support. I had no time to get in trouble with the law. I guessed he wanted to make up when I used to beat him in junior high. I never went back to the community center to play basketball.

My wife started applying for moderate rent months later, and we got accepted for an apartment. We moved into our new apartment. The building was new. Our apartment was on the seventeenth floor facing Tresser Boulevard. She got pregnant with our second daughter. She still was not working. I paid all the bills. We met some new friends in the building. Roger and I always saw each other at the bars, but we never went out together. His wife was a friend of mine. They love sewing their own clothes.

I did the laundry sometimes for my wife. One particular day, I decided to do the laundry. I was minding my own business, and this young lady approached me. She started talking to me. I was not thinking about cheating on my wife. She said, "I will grab your penis." I thought she was joking. I never heard any girls speak like that to me. All the girls I was raised around did not talk nasty. Where I was raised, the girls were decent. Mary grabbed my penis for real. I was stunned. This was new to me being twenty-one. I lost control of myself and got her apartment name. I failed in lust of the flesh. I lost focus on my marriage. I started going places with her. I lost focus on church. Mary's apartment face the parking lot. She was watching me every time I came home. I had no idea she was watching me. She waited for the right time to catch me alone. She finally caught me alone in the laundry area in the basement. She took me to a hotel. She paid for it. We had sex that night for the first time and another time at the beach in the back of my car. Policemen almost caught us in the act. We had it a few more times. During that time, my wife and I had fights because she suspected something was not right. I did not like Mary at all and had no feelings for her. It was all lust. I went to gambling houses and clubs with her. I did not like those places. I finally told her I was finished hanging out with her. I walked away from the relationship and never looked back. I moved out of the building to another low-income project. I regretted getting involved with Mary. This was the biggest mistake I ever made in my life. I never cheated anymore during our marriage. I stayed faithful the next three years.

We continued going to church. We started focusing on getting our education. We came to the conclusion she could go back, and I would go back after. She started going to design school in New York City. She started in September of 1978. It was a nine-month course. I had to stay on top until she finished school because she had her responsibilities with my two daughters. She had to come home to cook. It was taking a toll on her having all those responsibilities. She did complete the nine-month course. She graduated in June 1979 and started looking for a job.

She got her first job in Stamford. She was good at her job, and she met some new friends on the job. She only talked about men. I did not think anything of it. She was always faithful when we started going together in high school. During the time she was going to school, she met this guy that gave her a business card to buy a distrib-utorship in the company. I took out a loan to buy into the company. Isis Industries market shampoo for hair and lotion for your skin. I sold the products to beauty salons and stores and door-to-door. It did not work out because I quit my job. I was using all the money to pay the bills. I gave it up and found another job. My sister company hired me to do office work. I took the job. We were doing great.

She never stopped talking about the guys on her job. One day, when I finished work, I went home. She usually got off by 6:00 pm, and it started getting late. She never stayed out at night. I called her mother, and the children were at their grandparents' house. Mother had no idea, and her best friend knew nothing about where she was at all. She never came home that night. I was worried all night that something probably happened to her. I still did not think she was with another man. I went to her coworker's house; she mentioned the street a lot in our previous conversations. I went the next morning to Franklin Street. I knocked on the door, and a guy answered. I asked him if he saw Val. He said she was down the street at his friend's house—and she was there. She spent the night.

The marriage was over at that point. I did not trust her anymore. I lost my feelings for her. She was cheating with her coworker. My wife continued to cheat over and over again. Somehow I was connected to her designing. She lost her job. I hid my pain by giving her professional fashion shows. I gave two shows and walked away from the business. I tried to forget. The marriage ended after five years. We spent the next four years separated but still having sex, until I decided to end the sex. After nine years, the divorce was finalized. She wanted her maiden name back, and she gave me custody of my daughters.

So I got married again. I was ready to settle down. I stopped going to church. I did not want a life with different ladies. I never tried to hurt these women intentionally, but it happened. It was my life because there never seemed to have been any faithfulness among all the men in my life. My father never had that manly talk with me about how to treat a woman. He was too busy disrespecting all the women in his life. He never knew the true meaning of love. All his sons followed his path of unfaithfulness. I never wanted to be like him, I wanted something better for me. So I made a promise to God that if he returned my daughters back, I would be a better husband the next time. I would work harder understanding the next relationship.

After my separation from my wife, she told me many times I could not please her sexually after committing adultery with her lover. So I started reading more books on sex, how to please a woman, which body parts to turn her on as a woman. In some way, she got into my head. I actually thought sex was the problem why she was cheating, but it was not at all the problem. Married or separated, she kept coming back to engage in sex for nine years until the divorce was finalized. I made one last mistake with her. I had sex with her again while living with my girlfriend. We went to a hotel to finalize the divorce. My intention was to discuss how to save the marriage; hers was to have sex. We did have sex for the last time, but after the sex, she wanted to finalize the divorce the next day, on Monday. During that time, I probably would have left my girlfriend for my marriage. No matter how many years went by, keeping the family together was still my first priority. I wanted to make sure I was making the right decision. The next day, I met her at court to finalize the divorce. She had a lawyer, and I did not have an attorney. Judge Ryan granted us the divorce. There was no property to fight over, so the judge granted me custody and gave her maiden name back to her. As soon as we left the courthouse, she wanted me to go to New York City to get us a hotel to have sex. I said to her it was over. I never looked back. We had the discussion in the past that if we ever divorced, I was not looking back. I finally never cared about her again. All feeling was gone. Now I had to focus on my relationship with my girlfriend and daughters. There was no turning back.

I was honest with my girlfriend about what took place at the hotel. I did admit about having sex with my wife. I am always being honest and telling the truth. I was never a person to lie. The only conceivable sin in my life was fornication and adultery. I inherited those bad habits from my parents. I promised God I will allow him to free me from the lust of the flesh. Ms. O and I worked on our relationship. I moved out of my room and moved into her apartment. I was not honoring my Christian values. I was already living with my girlfriend while the divorce proceedings took place. My daughters were already living with me and my girlfriend before the divorce was finalized.

I did office work. I always got jobs as a data entry clerk. I went back to school to study computer science at PSI Institute in New York City. I met some new friends. I graduated in 1980 with a B average. I always got good grades in Stamford High School. I made the honor roll the last year of school. My ex-wife also said I was not smart enough after she got her certificate. I kind of believed it, but after years have passed, I realized she never got good grades in school. I did prepare myself for college. I began to read all kinds of college books. When people would throw their college books away, I would take them out the garbage and read them at home. After our conversation on the phone, I spent time educating myself. I had always been a step ahead of her.

I always had a job while living with my girlfriend. I was not putting my responsibilities on my girlfriend. I gave her money for rent and other bills. We both bought my daughters school clothes. I asked Ms. O. to marry me for the second time. This is my first time asking someone to marry me. The first time was arranged by her family even though I do not regret it. I learned something from the marriage. I learned to be a responsible person. My second wife's father witnessed the justice of the peace marrying us.

My ex-wife filed the divorce documents October 9, 1982. The divorce was finalized on August 10, 1982. The last time we lived together was the year 1980. During that year, she moved into her mother's house, and we continued giving professional fashion shows to get her some exposure in the design world. The first show was at the Italian Center in High Ridge in Stamford, Connecticut, and the final show the same year was at the Palace Theatre in New Rochelle, New York. After that, I never gave any more fashion shows for her, then she left town with my daughters. I continued to work and, I saw this ad in the paper about computer science. I contacted the school, PSI Institute. I registered in September that fall and graduated the same year with a B average. I registered with local agencies and found sturdy work as a data entry operator. Our relationship was still rocky. Six months later, after the divorce, I married my second wife, and the children were living with us. I was starting life all over again. Things were going well.

I thought after the divorce she would move forward with her life. I thought she was happy with her new life but was not at all. My new wife took good care of my children, and they went to school every day nicely. Their hair was well-groomed going to school. My oldest had problems handling the divorce, but I assured her she would be fine. Her sister was too young to understand. I made sure I protected my daughters. They were my world now. I had to deal with discipline. I had to fill those shoes as a mother. I never taught them against their mother even though she showed no interest but on herself. So I continued my new life as a father.

But I started learning new things about my wife that I did not know before I married her. She and her brothers did hard drugs. She seemed like she had it together, but she did not at all. One day, I came home to relax, and I noticed her and brother had this powder stuffed in aluminum foil. It was cocaine. I never did drugs at all. I asked them to remove it and leave. They all left the house. I never saw it anymore in the house. We continued to raise my children. Everything was moving along well. We both worked hard on our jobs. She did hair at a beauty shop. She did an excellent job doing my daughters' hair. I thought all the drama with my ex-wife was over since she had her life back. She found out later that my daughters were well taken care of by their stepmother. She did not like it at all because she was not doing anything for her daughters, so she started feeling guilty.

My second wife and I decided to move to Virginia to live. So I asked my oldest brother to find a storage place for our furniture. I borrowed my oldest brother's Electra 225, a Buick, to move my furniture, but going through New York and halfway on the New Jersey turnpike, the car broke down with a U-Haul on the back. I had to call my brother and father to come get us. So my brother and father had the car towed to the nearest gas station. My father paid to fix the car, and my other brother came and brought my furniture to Virginia and put the furniture in storage. We were going to get an apartment after and find a job. But more drama was added after my brother's car was fixed. My oldest brother got mad because I would not pay him again. He wanted to get paid twice. He always was crooked. He was never the most liable person to depend on at all. He took $700 from me to buy a car and never bought my car. I had to play cards with his crooked friends to get my money back and lost every card game. I will never play again. He refused to give my new car back to me. He was the most selfish out of all the siblings.

So he got mad at me and went back to my ex-wife to let her know I was moving out of town with the children. She was nowhere to be found at that time. I did not know where she moved in New Jersey. I had no clue if she was back living with her mother. All I knew was that I was being served a court document for custody of my daughters. She wanted to take the children from me to give to her mother. My ex-wife lied to the court regarding my wife and me about child abuse. She stated on the documents I was having sex with the children, and my wife was abusing my daughters. That was a low blow. I never expected she would go so low. She knew it did not happen. She did not want to see me happy. She was not happy with her life, so she pulled everyone into her mess. It was hard on my wife and me to go to court all through the year. We had to cancel our plans to move to Virginia, and my next oldest brother brought my furniture back to Connecticut.

So the court had to investigate the complaint. The court gave the children their own lawyer, and all parties had to get their own attorney. During the process, my wife and I moved out of her father's house into our own apartment. The court proceedings took a toll on my wife. The agency that investigated the complaint found out nothing happened to them; they had never been touched sexually by anyone. The children were well cared for by us. So the judge ruled in my favor, returning the children back to me. My own brother got on my ex-wife's side in court. He tried to tell the court I should not have my daughters. He was not a good example as an oldest brother. He could not handle me like the other siblings. He had no influence over me. I always had my own mind. I was different from my other siblings. I stayed to myself. The case was left open for a year. And my ex-wife and her new boyfriend came many times to pick fights with us, but I avoided any physical contact. If there was any fighting among us, the children would have been given to their mother. They were banking on me to slip up, but I understood why they kept it open—so they could give the children to their grandmother. Connecticut is a state that tries to help the mother keep custody of the children. I made sure my wife and ex-wife did not get in any fights before my children. That was a rough year for me dealing with this court situation.

I made it through their one-year probation, but it drove my wife deeply into cocaine. I found crack bottles in her jacket, and she was coming up short with money. She could not handle the pressure. She never mistreated my daughters. She always cooked dinner regardless of what was happening in her life. She was a good person and just had an addiction. Her brother had the same problem when we went to his house. They engaged together doing cocaine. I did not like her getting high, so I told her we were going home, and he jumped up and said she was not going anywhere with me. We got into a fight, and he lost the fight. She broke up the fight, and we went home. My wife's family were good people, and I never had any problem with them. They liked me.

After the one-year probation was finished, we moved to New York. We got married in February of 1984, and by New Year of 1985, we were separated, living in separate places. We went to her step-brother's house to celebrate New Year. Upon leaving, she kissed her brother in the mouth, and we drove back to New York and continued to argue. We were arguing so much the landlord called the police, and they asked my wife to leave. She never came back to live me. She came back to New York a few times but not to live. She started going out with this other guy and moved him into her father's house. We had sex a few times and decided to end it peacefully and remained friends. So I filed for a divorce in New York. I met someone else later. It was heartbreaking to lose both wives. I was hurting inside and stressed out, but I stayed strong for my two daughters. I had them to live for now.

I stayed to myself for six months, without getting engaged sexually with anyone. I needed time to myself. I went out on dates for fun but not to be close. It was hard not having sex. My body was used to having sex; now I was staying away from it. I was not living the Christian life or going to church. My body and mind took a beating after failing marriages. The marriage only lasted a year. I do not regard crying when she never came back after the first time. It was much easier to get it out of my system. It was over. I had no one to share this pain with because I was never close to my siblings. I never shared my feelings with any of them. I went to God even though I was not going to church. One thing I can say is that I was maturing as a young man. The mistakes I made with my first wife I did not make with my second wife. With my first wife, I would take her on vacation to Virginia and leave her with my mother and disappear. I would hang out with my childhood friends. And my brother and sister, on different occasions, would introduce me to girls. At the age of twenty-five, I had no self-control over my sexual appetite. By time I was twenty-nine, I had more control over it. I never cheated on my second wife. I was settling down. I wanted to be tied down to one woman. I never had any role models in my life. None of the men in my life ever talked about right and wrong or how to treat a woman. My father was too busy making outside babies. He had children with two different women while being with my mother. My brothers followed my father's behavior. They repeated the same act. They had outside children while being married to their wives. My first father-in-law went to New York every week. His wife dropped him on Friday and picked him up on Sunday for work on Monday. He was never faithful to his wife. My second father-in-law cheated on his second wife all the time. And my last father-in-law cheated all through marriage and had a girlfriend until he left his wife for his mistress. He had an outside baby while married. The only role model was my granddaddy, my mother's father. I had to learn from my first marriage how to be a good husband. I have always been a good father. I made a few mistakes that I will continue to write about.

My friend Charlie came into my life when I separated from my first wife. We met on the bus. He knows my life better than my sibling. He has been a great support to me. My other friend Jake was there for me. And Julie was there for me. She understands better than any woman. My first wife never brought abuse again until I met my third wife.

I met Jada again for the second time at the club. I was not looking for a wife. I met her the first time when another friend was giving a fashion show. We both were in the fashion show during my second marriage. I was signing divorce documents again. It was not complicated at all getting it over fast since we had no children. After the club was over, I asked Ms. Jada for a ride home. I left my car home that night. I was visiting my oldest sister with my daughters. My sister watched my daughters when I went to the club. Jada gave me her phone number, and I called the next day. We talked a lot on the phone. We got to know each other better. She would bring me food to my job that her mother cooked. She lived at home with her parents. We continued seeing each other, so I invited her to my apartment in. New York. I offered to cook her dinner.

After a few months, I moved back to Connecticut with my daughters. I applied for an apartment in housing. I had a friend that worked in the housing authority, and she put my application ahead of people. I moved into my new apartment with my daughters. I had full custody of them. It was strange being the mother and father, but I adjusted to fatherhood. I made a commitment to stand by my daughters. I always had some great mothers to watch my daughters while working. Sometimes I got on my bicycle to take my daughters to the babysitter. I was attached to them. I never asked their mother for any support. I fed them and clothed them. I made sure I helped them with their homework. I was still dating my girlfriend. My sister said it was not going to last, but we are still together after thirty six years.

My girlfriend got pregnant, and later, I asked her to marry me. By that time, we were living together. We both had good jobs. We did office work. On March 15, 1985, we got married by a justice of the peace. My ex-wife tried to stir up trouble again. She filed another document claiming child abuse again in court. I did not bother getting a lawyer. I represented myself at court. The court knew the allegations were false, and it was thrown out of court. Every time she broke up with her boyfriends or things were not going right in her life, she started claiming child abuse. She did not want me to be happy with my new wife.

When you care about human beings, you try to do the right thing. Love does not hurt. God put us on earth to love one another. No one plans for a divorce; it happens in life. Everyone dreams of making it last forever, but sometimes, it just does not work out that way. There are no winners in a divorce because the children get the short end of the stick in the end. Children want to be with both parents the way God made it. I tried to make it for the children regardless of mistrust and many mistakes by both us parents. I truly believed you should try your hardest to make it work. There is nowhere in the Bible it says that is the solution. The heart is selfish at times. I do not think divorce will actually solve the problems; it creates more problems. My ex-wives thought running away from their problems in life would be fine, but new problems were created. My first wife realized she gave up the most important part of her life: her daughters and, secondly, financial support. My second wife realized all the drugs could not replace a good man. It is hard to replace a good man or woman. I am not saying these women were bad wives, but they made bad choices. They did not prioritize what was really important, putting their selfish ambition before the family. Even though I made some bad choices, the family came first, especially what was best for the children. Marriage is the most complex thing God created among humans. All species have to deal with and protect the family. We all fall in moments when things are not going our way. And sometimes we get those days, and no one cares about us, but we cannot lose focus on the importance of the family. We must strive toward perfection. No two people will agree at all times, but most of the time they do. I never stopped trying to be the best I could be as a family man. I made some mistakes in my first marriage, but I corrected them in my second marriage.

Chapter 3

So I fell in love again, with my third wife. I was determined not to go through another divorce. It would be devastating to me. I decided to go back to my God for divine guidance. In order to survive this marriage, I needed to walk with God. I had to turn my life to my Creator. When I met my wife, I knew we would be together forever, but I had twice as much work to put into the marriage. She had all the qualities of a wife, but she could not control her emotions. She got out of control for no reason. I could not understand this type of behavior. It was hard for me because the other wives had lying and drug problems that were easy to comprehend. You can tell the lie between the truth and someone having a drug problem but do not know when a person is going to act out their emotion for no reason. This was the strangest thing I ever dealt with in my life. I remember when I first started going out with her, she scratched me for no reason. I did not take it to heart. I continued dating her and finally married her.

I noticed the difference between my previous in-laws and my new family. The new in-laws were always angry about something that was going on in their lives. The father never slept with his wife, always on the couch. And the father had a mistress that he continued to see. The wife was unhappy, but she fought to keep her marriage alive. My wife absorbed all that negative energy from her parents. She was not happy living there. I came along as her knight in shining armor. She was pregnant with our first baby, so I decided to marry her. I was happy about it. There are some reasons I love her after being with her. I told her I was going to buy her a house after three years. I bought our first house in Bridgeport, Connecticut.

But before I bought the house in Bridgeport, her brother tried to molest my daughter who was eleven at the time, and he was in his thirties. My wife called me to give the bad news, but my daughter had fought him off. I never expected this to happen to me. My daughter kept fighting him and kept her legs close. Once she mentioned my name, he stopped attacking her and left my house. He turned himself to the police. Later that day, the police called me to see if I wanted to press charges against him. I pressed charges, and he went to jail for a long time. I was disappointed in my wife because she never told me her brother went to jail in the past for raping his son's mother. I survived it. It could have put a strain on my marriage. I committed myself back to God, and it made it easy to forgive him. If I had known he would not have babysat my daughters.

The biggest mistake I made was that I did not get help for my daughter. I should have gotten her counsel. I did not think she needed it. I was so wrong. If anyone reads this book, believe your children and get them the necessary help. Always talk to your children and grandchildren if anyone touches them inappropriately. In Black families, molestation happens among family members. We have been brainwashed that it only happens with the Caucasian race. That is a big lie. My advice is do not put all your trust in family members. Observe them the same way as investigating a stranger. It took me a long time to get over the situation. It did affect me. I could never trust him again. Through the grace of God, I never hated him. God gave me the victory. He served his time in jail for the crime he committed, but he could never be trusted around any of my children anymore. He never told his mother the truth. He lied to his mother that he never did it. I told his mother my daughter is no liar. He turned himself in to the authorities, and I went to the police station to press charges. Until this day, I am not family to him because he never apologized for what he did to my daughter. He is never allowed to be in my house while my daughter is there. She was not comfortable being in his presence again. My wife and I got past this situation.

I thought things were moving along well until she told me she was going on a trip to visit her ex-boyfriend, people. I tried to talk her out of it. I did not think it was a good idea because he lived there, but she went anyway. It just did not look right to me. I never distrusted her, but anything could happen. It took me a while to forgive her. I was not a Christian at this point. Her friend was using her. I felt his sister was using my wife. My wife's friend rented a car for the trip and was supposed to drive it to Virginia. Instead, she drove my wife's car and left the rental with my mother-in-law. Later, her friend's mother came and got the rental car. This was a mess. In the process, my wife's engine blew up, and I had to go there with my friend to get her. The ex-boyfriend had to drive with her to take the car to an auto mechanic shop. We just had the baby when this happened. It was rocky, and I hung out at the club every week. Sometimes I came in the next morning. She was not happy with me staying out late. Her going down south affected me.

After three years of being married, we bought a house in Bridgeport. I was slipping back into my old ways. I was staying out all night. I was coming in the next morning. It was getting bad. I was messing up again. I came home with a hickey on my neck, and she questioned me. I told her a lie and said I got into a fight with someone at the club. She threw baby powder on my brand-new car the next morning. But the subject never came up again. My grandmother told me never tell the truth that does not work for me. I am not a liar; the truth will come out soon or later.

After her trip to Virginia, that's when we bought a house in Bridgeport. We were having our second child now. We put away our differences and moved forward with life. I always loved her, but I was trying to deal with her misplaced anger from her childhood, the things she experienced from her childhood. I started to understand why she was so angry. Her father made it known he loved his older daughter more. My oldest brother-in-law told me that when we first started dating. I saw the good side of her from her mother. Her mother was committed to her marriage regardless of what pain she was going through with her unfaithful husband. My wife had those qualities, sticking to her husband at all cost.

In our new house, my son came into the world. My wife kept the baby in Stamford, Connecticut, and she worked in Stamford.

She commuted back and forth to Stamford. She got pregnant before we moved to our new house. I was working as a messenger driver. I stopped hanging out in the clubs and started settling down with my four children. My wife stayed in Stamford a lot with the younger children at her mother's house because of her job, so we agreed on the arrangement. I spent more time with my oldest daughters. I was still responsible for managing my oldest daughters from a previous marriage I had sole custody of. I had to make sure they went to school and ate every day. I was responsible for all the discipline, not my wife. It was time when I had to discipline them. They did not agree with the way I chastised them, but I did my best. I did put them in the basement when they disobeyed my orders. I admit there were fleas in the basement. It was only for that night. I did chastise my oldest daughter for disobeying me three times. I did use a tree branch. Her mother called an agent about the situation, but nothing happened to me. I explained that I gave her three chances to correct her behavior. I had a certain time when they should be in the house. My mother raised me like that. She gave us a certain time to be in the house, or we were punished. I did not want my daughters having a life as a criminal. I did my best at that time being solely responsible as a father. I had no choice because their mother had no control of them when they visited her. The girls walked all over her. She could not handle them when they came home when they wanted to. My best friend would see them on the other side of town at night. I wanted the best for my daughters. I did my best at that time.

Now my third child was on the way. My wife was pregnant again by the time I was baptized. You could never understand love until you realized how you hurt someone else. I understood my first wife's bitterness toward me. She was hurt so many times in the relationship. That is the reason I could never hate her, but I have to move on to a better life. That is the reason I tried to understand my second ex-wife's feelings. I was working harder to be a better man, with more understanding, with my new wife. After my son was born, I accepted Jesus in my life. The Lord spoke to me and said, "Come out of the night to the light." I needed a higher power to control my life. I never meant to hurt any woman in my life, but it happened. I was still enjoying life with my new wife and five children in Bridgeport. After a few years, we moved back to Stamford because of high traffic of drugs. I was not planning on it, but my wife said her father walked out on her mother. And she wanted to know if I wanted to take over her mother's house in order for her mother to have a place to live. I said yes because I did not want to raise my children in an infested neighborhood. Year later, we moved back with the two children. My oldest daughters were old enough to live with their mother.

After we got settled, I had to bring the mortgage up to date. I called the mortgage company to make arrangements to settle the debt. I made arrangements with an attorney to have her parents quit-claiming the deed to me and my wife to protect my interest in the matter because her father could not be trusted. I was not going to take the gamble trusting his word. I knew anytime once I caught up, he would come back and put me out. But the downfall was my wife never told me about the back taxes on the house. It was not a happy situation taking over the house. My wife's father started poisoning his wife, saying I was trying to take the house from them when he walked away from the house. I was miserable living in that house because they made me feel like I was the bad guy, and I was trying to help her mother. It was a total nightmare the whole time living there. I stayed in the streets. Every weekend, I disappeared, but I always went to church every Sabbath. I never gave up on God in my bad situation. My wife was always on her parents' side. I had a choice to stay in that house and divorce my wife or leave it with my wife. Now she was pregnant again. She was carrying my fourth child at the time of her oldest brother's death. She conceived during time. Out of all my fathers-in-law, my wife's father is the worst. All my previous fathers-in-law came to my wedding except her father. The only comment was his daughter was going to turn me into a drunk. This was a total insult. He never came to our wedding, and we lived down the street. As a matter of fact, none of her siblings came, only her mother, but my family came to give me their blessing. After that, we never wasted our time any more cooking. My wife's father is the worst father-in-law I ever had in my life. The first two were good.

Some more drama entered into my life. I was messing up after the second year of marriage to my third wife. I was going out to clubs every week. At that time, I did not care about the marriage for some reasons. I fell back into my old tricks going with this girl. I did not love her, just hanging out. Something was missing in my life. My wife was frustrating me for no reason. She stayed angry for no reason before I started hanging out. She was the most difficult person I ever dealt with in my life. I think she had her own issues from the past; she never freed herself. She has always been a productive and faithful wife, but she could not control her emotions. Hanging out was my way of dealing with the pain.

I was still having problems with my older children. Their mother would try to pick fights when visiting my house. One time she tried to force herself in my apartment. We got into a physical fight. She scratched me on the neck, and she got a little scratch on her. She called the police, and no one got arrested. We both had to appear at court. The court monitored us for a year, and the case was closed. It was the same situation I experienced with my second wife. She was trying to create the same atmosphere. She filed court documents again about child abuse, but she left my third wife out of it. The court dismissed the allegation because they knew it was false.

After my first child with my third wife was born, a new situation occurred. We did not have a babysitter that week. My wife's mother usually watched the baby, but she had something to do, so she asked her son. My wife and I had to work, so her brother watched the baby, and my eleven-year-daughter was there. I got a phone call later that day that her brother tried to rape my daughter. I was angry and left my job. My daughter fought her attacker off, and she started screaming telling him, "I am going to tell my father." She kept her legs closed while screaming. I had no idea until after the incident when he went to jail for rape. This was a hidden secret. I went to downtown Stamford to press charges against him. My new brother-in-law turned himself in to the police before I got home. The agency tried to offer me help for my daughter. I refused the help. Most Black men deal with their own problems. I was one of them. In the long run, I did not help my daughter. This was my first biggest mistake. I will tell you why it was a big mistake not to get help when it happened. I did not think she needed help. I was so wrong at the time. We never talked about it again. My advice to anyone who experienced an attack on your children, get help. It did affect me a little, but I prayed to God not to hate him. It took me years to get it out of my system. I completely forgave him for his wrongdoing. After he served about ten years in jail, I was completely healed. After he got out of jail, I came in contact with him at another family members' houses. I never spoke on the topic. It did come across my mind at times, but I never pursued it. I was hoping he would apologize for his action. But later down the years, he tried to tell his mother that my ex-wife told my daughter to accuse him of child molestation. He was still lying to his mother. After, he did rape a White girl and did more years in jail. His mother and family knew he was a rapist. I was never close to him because I just married my wife. It had only been two years when it occurred. He drove me farther from him. He was never allowed around my children at any time, not even to visit when I am not home. He would only be in my presence or my wife's, never alone anymore.

After two years, we bought a house in Bridgeport, twenty miles from Stamford. It was a quiet street and a nice house. By that time, I was doing messenger work and stopped doing office work. I was making more money driving each week. I was on the road six days a week, approximately sixteen hours a day. I did not drink that much, only on the weekends. My wife and I got baptized at Seventh Day Adventist Church before my son was born. My wife stayed in Stamford most of the time while I took care of my oldest daughters. We did agree on that arrangement since she worked in Stamford, but in the long run, it was not good for the relationship. Even though I stopped going to bars and clubs, I slipped back into adultery. I did it a few times and stopped. I was like a person rebelling again but for different reasons. It was not her uncontrollable temper because I accepted her behavior. But by her not being home, I was weakened again. I was still going to church. We did not have a strong commitment on keeping the Sabbath. We disagreed all the time. Observing it, I was accustomed to keeping the day holy. It was unknown to her. After years went by, it grew on her, but I struggled with her spiritually. It was hard to get her to pray with me or read the Bible together. I was lonely spiritually. It is hard when you are not in harmony. But through the grace of God, he kept us together.

Now she was pregnant with our third child. I got back on track again. I started focusing on God and church. I was still plagued with the lust of the flesh, but I kept asking God to deliver me from that demon. It was not easy for me dealing with my wife's and children's problems, trying to keep my daughters on the right path. They were becoming teenagers which made it harder. No one knew actually what I was going through as a husband and father. It was not my wife's job to discipline my daughters, and their mother was no help at all because when they visited their mother, she could not control them, and my wife was not involved in that aspect of the relationship. Life had always been complicated sticking by my daughters at all cost, but I tried to be the best father I could be at that time. My way of discipline was not always agreeable with my daughters, but when they got in trouble in school or out of school, I was there. I never gave up being a good father.

After becoming a deacon and Sabbath schoolteacher, my parenting skills improved. I changed the way I disciplined my other children. The more I got involved with the church, the more I was maturing as a man. My wife continued to travel back and forth to Stamford and Bridgeport. My wife experienced some of her own changes learning to be a stepmother. This was not easy for her. I did not expect a lot from her when it came to my daughters. She had to deal with a nine- and eleven-year-old. She had no experience in managing my daughters and dealing with two more children of her own. She had her hands tied. By that time, she was dealing with a two-year-old and a five-year-old and teenagers and traveling up and down the highway. I did not put too much pressure on her. By the time we had our third child, the neighborhood was becoming drug infested, and people were shooting guns every night. It was not a good place to raise children, but we dealt with the situation. I tried to report the drug dealer to the police, but it was a disaster. I called the police to make a complaint that I did not want the person selling drugs in front of my house. Somebody at the police station informed the person I made a complaint. The person came at me with a pipe, but his friend stopped him and said I was a good guy and to leave me alone. I never had a problem with them anymore. I knew it was time to walk away from that house. The drug dealers were destroying people's properties, and the value of the houses was dropping.

My wife's mother and father were losing their house, so my wife suggested we move there. My oldest daughter graduated before we made the transition and went to college, and her sister got emancipated at sixteen. She moved to her mother's apartment. Our third child was born after we moved to my wife's mother's house. I moved back to Stamford, and her parents quitclaimed their house to my wife and me. By that time, her father moved into his mistress's house and left his wife with all the financial burden. Her father moved out before we moved in the house. Her mother had no job, so we tried to stop the house from going into foreclosure. I spoke to the bank and brought the mortgage up to date, but my wife never told me back taxes were owed on the property, and the city had a lien on it. She had a way of keeping me in the dark about things. This is another problem I had to deal with, the city taxes. It was already filed in court before I moved into the house.

There was another bad situation I had to deal with at the time. When her brother came to visit his mother, he made it known he did not like me living there. He would speak to me, and their father also came back trying to confuse the situation by having his daughter call a meeting with me. I did not want to talk to him about why I made them sign documents to protect me. My wife did not care because it was her parents. I had to protect myself. As time passed, my mother-in-law called her brother to tell me how to run the affairs of my house. They all made it known I was not appreciated there. My mother-in-law made it known in my presence that I stole the house from her when I tried to help her from leaving the house. They all forgot the husband made the mess, and I tried to correct it. I felt like a stranger in that house full of demons. I was never happy there, so by the time my daughters were born, I never stayed there on the weekends. I stayed at the clubs and went to church in the morning. I never missed church. My wife stopped going to church for a while, and before, she often went with me. I was a lonely man.

I had some more drama to the situation. I met a girl downtown, and she stopped me. She asked me my name, and I told her my name. She said, "This girl named Dale had your baby twenty-one years ago, but she never contacted you about the child." I said I knew Dale. She wanted to know If I wanted to meet the young lady. I met Dale twice at her house, and she came to my house the next week to have sex. I never saw Dale again. I remember months later, she wanted money for an abortion. She never contacted me anymore when I refused to give her money for an abortion. I never saw Dale pregnant. That was my last conversation with her, on the phone. I did get the number from the lady. I claimed her as my daughter, which is my third biggest mistake. As I write I will explain why it was a bad decision. I should have taken a DNA test before I got involved with her life.

The second mistake I found is that my first born by my current wife was molested by a family member. My own nephew used to change his diapers. One day, I was hugging my wife. My nine-year-old did not like it, and I sat down and asked her if anyone ever touched her in the wrong place. She said it was her cousin. I asked her which cousin. She said Tom took her out of the room in the middle of the night and wet on her. I said, "Your baby cousin's father has the same name." She said the father did it, not the son. I contacted him by phone because he lived in Virginia, and I was in Connecticut. I asked him why he did that to my daughter, and he denied it. And he asked me who I was going to believe, him or my daughter. I said I believed my daughter. And I warned my brother not to let their children stay at his house. I contacted my mother and father about it to get their advice on how to handle it. They both said let God handle it, so I did not press charges. This was the second biggest mistake I regret in my life. I should have gotten counsel from someone experienced in handling these types of problems. I was never close to my nephew after this happened, but I still mingled because there were always times when the whole family got together, but I would never allow my daughter to be in the same location with him. Until this day, I do not know if my parents' advice was good for me and my daughter not to have him arrested or report it. My oldest daughter from my first marriage was molested by my current wife's brother. I failed to get proper counseling for both daughters. When both daughters became adults, they said they were affected by those men.

After nine years, we traveled to Virginia. My daughter stayed with their girl cousin, and the other children stayed with us. I never confronted my nephew again about the matter. He had a track record for disrespecting his wife. He tried it with his wife's girlfriend before moving back to Virginia. He created a wedge between our relationship, someone I trusted with my life. Now all those years being his uncle went to waste, but I still could not hate him. I was taught by my grandmother to never hold a grudge no matter how it hurts. "The Lord will fight your battle." My mother and father repeated the same verse in the Bible. Sometimes we cannot see bad things coming our way, but God prepares us to stay strong. Every time I came in contact with him, it came back to my memory. There were times I could feel he was trying to make peace with me but just could not admit to his wrongdoing to my daughter. I truly believe time heals all wounds if you give it to God. If I did not have the love of God in me, I would not have forgiven those family members that attacked my daughters. It is not always the stranger you have to be concerned about but your own flesh and blood. Since all these happened, I do not trust my grandchildren around these family members. My children and grandchildren are my pride and joy. This is the main reason I work hard. My wife and I moved past the abuse done to my daughters.

My wife was now pregnant with our fourth child. The timing was slightly off because her oldest brother passed away; he became very ill. It was a sad time for me because I liked him. He gave me some information about how her first boyfriend treated her. She was abused by him. My wife had her own problems, not being treated equally with her oldest sister. Her father made it known to her she is not her favorite daughter; she was less than her sister. She came into our marriage with low self-esteem. She carried that burden for a long time. My brother-in-law shared that information with me along with her sister's husband. My sister-in-law's husband was drunk all the time. He could not stop drinking. He always went to work drunk. He was not that involved in raising his children because of his condition. He was a good provider. He always treated me with respect, but he lowered his position in his household. She dominated him. She took control of their relationship. She was the decision maker. It took him years to recover from his addiction. He finally signed up for a program to save his job. But it was too late to instill values in his sons and daughter. My in-law's son never grew up. My father-in-law's favorite was less successful. I remember my wife and I took her sister to New York every year for school shopping. You never know how much they really feel about it until some years have gone by. I knew my wife's twin brother did not care too much about his actions. Later, my daughter heard him talking about me, how he could not stand me. This is a person I lent child support to. I kept him out of jail. This is the thanks I received from him. I lent my sister-in-law money to pay her rent, and she was telling her daughter's boyfriend she did not approve of me marrying my wife and thought I was better than her family. All I wanted was more for my family. I tried the mail-order business but failed, but I finally got it right when I started my home improvement business. I started going to college to better myself. It was not easy juggling business, family, and church duties. It was hard for me. I never got any support from my wife. She was negative about me going to college and starting my business. She wanted me to stay on a job, but I wanted more out of life. So I took a few college courses to get into the groove. I read the whole dictionary when I worked at this insurance company. I read plenty of college books in my early years. I always loved reading. I had to do it alone without my wife's support. It was hard not having your wife's support. I was my own man. She had always been around people that settled for less. I was always around people that wanted more out of life. My mother took a nursing course to do better. I learned from her to do better. My mother has always been my greatest inspiration.

Chapter 4

During that time, all my brothers and oldest nephew lived in Connecticut. It was a nightmare, all of them moving back to Connecticut. My two oldest brothers loved to gamble a lot. They both made good money; one installed carpet, the other had four stores. They both had the same thing in common—playing the field. My oldest brother thought he was untouchable with ladies. He always thought he had all the brains, but in the end, he got burnt. Both their wives left them for cheating. They were like my father, making outside children, only different. They loved beautiful cars. My oldest brother was always outwitted by his live-in girlfriend. He continued cheating on his girlfriend, and she got her a boyfriend. He thought he had her wrapped around his fingers. He was up for a big surprise. When he went out the front door, she went out the back. Her boyfriend was handsome and had a good job at the post office. He outwitted himself. He put her out, or she left him. All his girl-friends were leaving him for another man; they got the best of him. He was not that smart. He should have learned from his wife when she left him.

My next-oldest brother followed his path but did not care if they left him; he was just being fly. He wanted to do right but did not know how to do right. One time, my brothers were gambling, and they were arguing about who was cheating. I did not want to see them fighting, so I intervened to stop it. I remember when I was in high school, they got into a fight about who was cheating. I got between them to stop the fight and almost got stabbed by a knife. My oldest brother got cut and was rushed to the hospital. He stayed in the hospital for days to heal. I did not want the same situation to repeat itself, so I got between them a second time and got into it with my oldest brother. He came toward me, and I gave him a karate kick. After that, I got back into my van and tried to leave, but my sister jumped on my van to help my oldest brother, and I almost ran him over because he got in front of it. I was dragging my sister, and she finally let go. I never hung out with them anymore, It was too much drama for me. O was not used to it. After that, my next-oldest brother moved back to Chicago. He got married for the second time to a younger lady his daughter's age that did not last long at all. They lived together in Connecticut but later married in Chicago. She later died on drugs.

And later, my baby brother, Alex, moved to Chicago, and my nephews moved back to Virginia. Years later, my baby brother was shot in Chicago. He tried to intervene for my nephew. My nephew was in an argument with some guy at the pool hall and threatened the guy with a gun. My brother was home when my nephew called him, and he left home to defend my nephew. My baby brother never did listen to my mother; she always had trouble with him. The gunshot messed his whole inside, and half his stomach had to be removed. We all prayed that God would spare his life. He came through with all the surgery. My mother and stepfather went out to Chicago to give their support, and my father went also. After he gained his strength, he went to live with my mother and stepfather. After all that happened, he still did not do good by my mother. They fed him and housed him, and when he received his money, he never gave my parents anything. They asked him to leave their domain. Later, he decided to move back to Connecticut to my sister's house. He continued to use drugs and abuse his body. He had to live the rest of his days with a bag to dispose of his waste. My sister could not handle him. He never gave her money. He spent his money on sex. My sister put him out; she has always been close to him all her life. They enjoyed the same things, smoking and getting high on drugs, marijuana, something I did not engage in. So he asked me if he could stay in my basement. The whole family warned me not to let him move into my house, but I could not turn him down, but we did get a good understanding about the rent. He paid me faithfully. I had only one problem, when he demolished my garage doors. He gave me a raggedy van that broke down while I was driving. And he wanted me to fix it. I refused to fix it; everything under the hood was rigged. The van was already in bad shape. I never borrowed anything from him again. I wanted to kill him for demolishing my garage doors. I went down to Bridgeport to check the damages. My wife's cousin called me about the doors. I confronted my brother about the garage doors, and he picked up an iron rod to hit me. I left the basement to avoid something bad happening, and he followed me outside to my car. I got in my car and left. He tried to get in front of the car to stop me from leaving. The next day, he tried to apologize and fixed the garage doors. I said no to him and fixed it myself. He had always been mean to me, but I avoided it. One thing I can say is he could make you laugh. Later, he got sick and went into the hospital. He stayed in the hospital for about a year, and then died. We got to know each other spiritually. I read the Bible to him every week and prayed with him. Before he left St. Vincent, he did agree not to agitate me anymore. He stuck by his word. I found out why he picked on me all the time. He admired me for living a Christian life and being committed to my family.

My sister, one year older than me, left to live with my grand-mother at an early age. My mother thought it would be best for my grandmother to raise her because of the five boys. I know my mother thought she was making the right decision during that time, but it affected me and my sister. She missed being raised by Mother and watched my mother raise her stepdaughter. My sister had a lot of bitterness from past scars. I should have been close to my sister, but it never happened because she left to live with my grandmother. I was much too young to understand, but I realized the wedge between us. I had always been a loner growing up, but it made me stronger and wiser than the rest morally. My sister had always been close to my younger brothers and oldest brothers. I had to stand alone. My sister and oldest brother carried grudges for life; they did not know how to let go of past grievances. My sister was hurt by her first boyfriend and was not a person to accept rejection. She lashed out violently. She tried to cut him, and she finally got over the situation. She treated her boyfriends like gold but was always underappreciated. She fell in love again with this guy in a singing group and married him right away. It did not last over a month; he vanished in the blue sky. They call him Flee, and that's just what he was as a person. He never stayed in one place. She was madly hurt again. She experienced the worst luck in keeping a man. I was married to my first wife when her husband disappeared for life. Years later, she divorced him. I felt sorry for my sister losing love again. This was the first time I witnessed her loneliness. She bounced back with her life. She had a son by this guy that forced her to have sex around fifteen that contributed to some of her bitterness. She is the only sister I spent years around during my childhood and adult life.

I had other sisters on my father's side and stepsisters from my mother's marriage. I never met one of my sisters; I just heard about her. The other sisters lived far away from me. My sister Jill opened up her doors for me and my daughters to live with her after we came back from California. It was the right decision for my daughters. If I did not bring them home, their future would not have been promising. They would have grown up on welfare, and most children raised on welfare have low self-esteem about life. I made sure that would not happen. After I met my third wife, my sister said it would not last, but we were still together when she met her second husband who was the age of her son. She treated him like a king. She brought his food every day to her bedroom and had his clothes laid out for the next day. This lasted a long time, about five years, until he met another woman. She never told me he left her for another woman; he told me. She was sad again. She loved him. I thought she was doing too much for him. She gave the man no breathing space. This was the second Spanish guy to walk out on the marriage.

I was holding on to my wife. I added some more drama in my wife's life claiming this girl to be my daughter. She was twenty-one at the time. My other daughters were grown and no longer living with us. I knew nothing about her. I did not know she existed. The last conversation I had with her mother was when she wanted money for an abortion, and I refused to give her money for the abortion, I was only eighteen during that time and only met her mother twice. Months later, she wanted to get rid of it. I never saw her pregnant and never saw her again. My wife was against me claiming the girl unless I took a DNA test, and she was right, but I did not listen to her. So later, after I met her, I did things for her. She was convinced by her mother I was her father. I asked her what her mother told her about me. She said her mother told her I wanted an abortion and did not want her.

I responded back by telling her, "Your mother lied to you." So I asked her, "Where is your mother so I can straighten out this lie?"

She said her mother was in jail and had about a year to complete. After that, I introduced her to my other grown daughters and the rest of the family. This is another mistake; I regret not listening to my wife. I got involved with her personal life. She had two children at the time and a deadbeat boyfriend. She had her own apartment, taking care of her children and sisters because the mother was in jail. She never called me by my name, always Dad. As time passed, I accepted I was her father without the DNA. I treated her like the rest of the children. I had no bias, but she wanted more as a father. She wanted to be treated special over the other children. My oldest daughter was not that receptive to her because they were close in age, and she had always been my oldest, but the one next to the older one was receptive to her.

My half-sister that I met for the first time when I was married to my second wife asked me to come to her friend's party, and I took my daughter from my first wife and her sister from another woman. My new daughter showed herself and wanted to go back to Connecticut. She could not wait for me to take her back. She called somebody to come get her and my daughter. I was not leaving New York; I just arrived at the party. I left later that night. I never spoke on the subject again about her behavior. As time passed, she wanted me to look at her car. It needed some work on it, so I checked it out. It was an old Ford. She was in her first semester of college when I met her, and she was going to drop out. I came along when she needed a father. The man she was raised by was on his way to jail for drug trafficking. He was about to do it for at least ten years after her mother got out of jail.

50

He had two daughters by her mother, and the court never let both parents do time at the same time. So I got to know her as a person, but I made it clear I was not trying to make up for lost time. "It is not my fault your mother lied to you," I told her. I was in Stamford, Connecticut, in my car park, and this lady I went to high school with came to my car. "Sue had your baby. Do you want to meet your daughter?" I never knew about the child. She was twenty-one when I met her. None of my wives and I had any idea she existed. Her mother was never going to contact me anyway. My daughter came to me later, asking me to cosign for a new car. I still did not take a DNA test, but I did sign under one condition: she paid for the car. I did not tell my wife because it would be an argument because there was no proof she was my daughter. I kept that a secret for a long time but finally told my wife. I normally do not cosign for my children unless they finished college, but she was an exception to the rule.

I continued living life, but things were still shaky at home. I was not happy moving into her parents' house. It was a nightmare every week. I would go out every Friday and Saturday night. I was drinking and going out with this girl. I never loved her, just trying to escape reality. It was a bad situation dealing with abuse from her family. I worked at night delivering papers and during the daytime, after working all night, my wife had a tendency to pick fights. I guessed she was angry too. She had no reason, just could not control herself. What kept us together is I always loved her and loved being around my children. I am not the type of man to walk away from my marriage. She would have to do it. I believed in keeping the family together at all cost. I knew in order for me to save our marriage, I had to walk away from that house. I felt so empty living there. Now my wife was having our fourth baby. Now the city was bringing us to court about taxes, and the court attorney was not backing off. I did not have enough financial support to bring taxes up to date. Things were on me, and I had no one to share this problem. I was on track as long as her father was giving us money for his wife. She had no job or income at the time. I could not cut it. I came to the conclusion to move out of the house. So I stopped paying the mortgage and started putting that money in the bank every month. It took the court a year to foreclose on the house. I had nothing to lose by walking away from it. I had to protect my family financially. The court finally foreclosed on the house and gave us time to move out. By that time, her mother moved into the senior citizen building. My wife's father bought a house with his mistress down south, and after a year, he moved back to Connecticut to a room. I never heard anything about his mistress anymore, and his wife had her own place.

I looked in the local newspaper and found an apartment in Norwalk, Connecticut. I only saw my extended family once in a while; I was too busy working. My baby was born in January, and the year after, we moved into our new apartment. I made an agreement to fix it for the landlord to adjust the rent. I was a carpenter and contractor. My son had his own room, and the girls shared a room. We had the master bedroom. We had a German shepherd dog. He had a doghouse in the back of the house. Before my daughter was born, I gave up the night life and asked God to straighten out my life. I had to focus on doing right by myself in order to help my wife.

My oldest daughters my wife and I raised visited us often, and we continued being part of their lives. My ex-wife was having a problem with my daughter going back to college, so she called me to have a talk with her. When my daughter was living with me, she got pregnant, and during that time, her sister broke the news to me. I got mad at the sister, and the funniest thing she said was that "I am not the one pregnant." By the time I saw my daughter, I gave her my support. But I made it clear, "I do not want you getting married because you are pregnant but to continue your education." She went straight to business college after graduation, and she completed two years. So the reason her mother wanted me to talk to her is because she stopped going to college to move in with her boyfriend with the baby. After I had a fatherly talk with her, she moved back into her mother's apartment with the baby, and she completed college. There were nights I had to go to her school to bring her home for breaks. My ex-wife knew I could get through to her. I raised her. I never had too many problems with my daughter. She was easy to get along with. But her sister was not the easy person to get along with at times. Both girls were smart when it came to learning. Her sister got pregnant later. She was emancipated, living on her own, but her mother wanted her to get married. I was totally in disagreement. My second oldest daughter wanted a place to stay at my house, but I said no because I was living in my wife's mother's house when we took over. I was already having problems with my wife's family, and the house was too small, so she went to live with her grandmother. She had a good relationship with her grandmother. She played part in raising her when her mother was in the jungle.

Once my wife and I moved into our new apartment, our relationship was getting better. I stopped the cheating and never looked back. My business was growing. Before I started my new business, I took a business course in college. I learned why I fell into my other businesses. I took the wrong approach. My professor talked about why most businesses fail in the first five years—because of lack of capital. From that point on, I became successful. I didn't quit my job like the first time. I worked at night to pay the household bills and used the profit to make the business better. I quit my day job and started my home improvement business. My wife did not give me any support. She was against it. She wanted me to work a job where she could not see my dreams. I grew the business, and I learned all the skills from my craftsmen. It was a struggle not having her support, but I got through it. It made me stronger each day. I had three business trucks. I was doing great, but something was missing. I needed more education. I decided to go back to school to get my associate degree. I worked day and night in my business and school. I juggled my business and school. It was rough managing my family and my church obligation. I had to teach Sabbath school and was a deacon. I lost money when I was in class because workers were slacking on the job. I had some great professors willing to give me the proper help. I graduated with a C+ average to make it to a four-year college in the future. We celebrated my graduation victory at a restaurant. My baby brother was proud of me. Bo loved taking pictures of everyone; that was his style. I began to focus more on family, so I decided not to go back to school right away until my children were grown, but I did inspire my two oldest daughters to continue their education. I moved from Norwalk to Bridgeport for the second time. My landlord did not want to compensate me for the repairs I did on his apartment. I decided to move out because his word was not his bond. He was not the most honest person.

I searched the papers and found an apartment in a nice neighborhood. I had the same amount of space. We continued going to church weekly, and I was still doing good in my business. I continued to save money. After a few years in that apartment, my new landlord wanted to sell me her condo. I agreed to buy it. I was sure my credit was enough to be approved, and I owed back taxes. She connected me to a real estate agency. The agent ran my wife's and my credit reports, and we were eligible for the loan. Once the landlord found out, she wanted to go up on the original price offered to us. I asked if we had to buy that place, and the agent said no. We started looking for a fixer-upper. I never bought my landlord's unit. My wife did not want to buy anything at the time, but I convinced her. We found a three-family house that needed work done to it. We closed on the building, and my workers helped me with the repairs. My oldest children grew up living their own lives. My wife and I moved into the new house with four children.

After moving into our house in 2003, more drama followed me. My oldest was in trouble, the younger was moving to Virginia, and my new daughter I claimed needed money for a house she wanted to buy. I did not tell my wife I was giving out all this money to my daughters. I knew she would not agree with my decisions, especially the new daughter I claimed. She had no problems with my other daughters because she helped me raise them. If I took the DNA test, the other daughter would have been accepted. I tried to keep some of my decisions to myself to keep the argument down. It was never easy trying to please everyone. She always supported my oldest daughter. I helped my daughter financially to move to Virginia. My friends and I helped load the truck for my daughter, and I drove it to Virginia. I gave money to my oldest daughter to help her to get out of her legal troubles. And the new daughter I met at twenty-one asked me to go to the closing of a house with her. I rode with her to South Norwalk to close on the house. We sat at the table with the lawyers, realtor to discuss the closing. The closing cost was $7,000 plus, and my daughter only had $1,000 to put on the house. She could not close the deal. I negotiated the deal for her. I asked the lawyers to work out a better deal for the closing. They said go, and they would call me later. I received a phone call later, and the price was dropped to $4,000 for the closing. That was not enough to make a deal, so I went back to the drawing board. I told my daughter to ask the realtor to take a cut on their commission. She called them, and they returned the call later reducing the closing to $3,000, and I went to the bank. I asked for a certified check for $2,000, and I gave it to my new daughter to take back to the lawyer for the closing. We drove back to the office and took the check inside to the lawyers, and she finalized the deal. She could not make the deal on her own because she lacked money and skills to close on the house. Once she moved into the house, all the doors were off the hinges on three floors. I hung all the doors with no charge. I always tried to help my children progress financially. My wife had no idea I gave my daughters all that money at once. She only knew about my daughter's legal expenses and daughter's moving expenses. She would have flipped on me if she knew I was helping this new daughter knowing I did not take a DNA test.

I kept another secret from her. After my last child was born in 1987, I got too involved with my new daughter and her affairs. After a few years passed, I never approached her mother about the lie she told her daughter regarding her birth. Her mother planted a lie on me that I did not want her, and I wanted an abortion. She believed that lie her mother told her. She held animosity against me even though I did all those things for her. She never accepted me as her father but wanted the material things I could give her. She never wanted a relationship with my other children, except for one that she could manipulate. She felt the girl was her sister. I did introduce her to the family as family. But my oldest daughter was not accepting her new sister like that at the time. She was puzzled that she came from nowhere, just out of the blue skies. She never opened up to her new sister. She stayed her distance from her. I never talked to my daughter about her before. I never knew she existed. I knew my ex-wife had something to say about their new sister because my granddaughter always disowned her as her aunt. My youngest children were much too young to understand the situation. As they got older, my wife told them she was not blood. I never dealt with it the right way. I passed the buck. I let too much time go by and did not straighten out the lie. After I bought my new daughter the house, I thought we were in good standing, but I was so wrong with my decision. That is why we should deal with matters right away; if not, it becomes nasty at the end.

I told my new daughter I would do anything for her out of kindness, but if I found out she was using me because of what her mother told her, she would see another side of me. I was not making up for lost time. She was twenty-one at the time I met her the first time and twenty-two when I cosigned for her first brand-new car. My new daughter was about twenty-five when I bought the house. A friend told me she did not accept me like the man she was raised by during her early years. The same lady that told me about my new daughter gave my friend the message to give me. I did not accept the gossip because I wanted to find out the truth. I wanted to find out myself if she said it. I was not trying to compare myself with anyone. I was only concerned about me not getting hurt by it. I wanted to give my new daughter a chance to prove herself. I did not want to pass judgment on her.

As the years were passing, it gave me a chance to know her as a person. She wanted me to turn against my daughters by siding with her when she was wrong. She asked her sister if her children could stay with her, and she would give money to feed them every week, but she went back on her agreement. She did not give her sister any money once they moved into her sister's house. My new daughter wanted my advice on the matter. I told her she was wrong, and her children were disrespectful. She had an attitude on the phone. She hung up the phone. I was not taking sides for no one, just being natural. She had an attitude with my other daughter about the noise in the apartment she was renting downstairs. She broke up with her live-in boyfriend, and now she was complaining she could not sleep because she had to go to church, but it was no problem when they were making noise. Now I see her nasty attitude about her sister. She told me she was taking her sister that was raised by me to court if she did not pay her rent. I said it was not necessary because she would pay her rent, and if there were any damages to the apartment, I would make all the repairs. I mediated between both of them. I did not want it getting out of control within them. My new daughter would have never taken her other sisters raised by her mother to court. She helped raised them while her mother did five to ten years in jail. The person I met in the beginning was not the same person, a hard working person. She had a dark side about her. Now I was seeing it. She had a lot of bitterness in her. She was angry with me because for twenty-one years, she was never in my life, but my other children were in my life. She was jealous of her new siblings. She was still blaming me for those early years even though I saved her from a bad life. She was going downhill when I met her. I gave her a real father. The man she was raised by was a drug dealer with no education or financial success. I had an excellent track record. I own my own construction business and was going to college. I was in a successful relationship with my wife and raised my children. I had no reason to abandon her as a child. It was her mother's choice not to have her father in her life.

Now there was another incident with her daughter and her sister's daughter. She wanted me to talk to my daughter about a ticket her daughter got in New York. My granddaughter used her cousin's name to get out of trouble. She claimed more money was due on the ticket. I told her I would discuss the matter with her sister, and I did get back to her. I called her on the phone and let her know I gave the message to her sister. There was nothing I could do about my granddaughter's behavior, but I let her know her daughter was wrong. I did confront the issue, and she was mad again with me. This was another case of love misinterpreted by my daughter. I could not make adults do anything they choose not to do. I tried to be a good father to a girl. I do not know if she is my blood, but I did all those fatherly duties. She wanted to turn me against my other daughters when she was wrong. I was trained as a deacon to examine both sides and be fair. My granddaughter was wrong using somebody else's identity. I made it clear to my daughter I was against it. She still had an attitude with me. I visited her children throughout the years and they never called me grandfather, just stared at me. I am quite sure more lies were told about me. My wife kept saying "she is using you," but I did it from the heart. The biggest lie was that I did not want her and wanted to abort her. Lies are usually passed down to the next generation when the person is hurt.

The only person she never had a problem with is my son, but my daughters could not handle that she was close to me. I tried to protect as much as I could as a human being and a new father. After she almost finished college, and I bought the house, she wanted to start her own day care on the first floor. My other daughter moved out, not owing her any rent money, and the apartment was in top shape. I did a thorough inspection to keep the peace among them. My daughter left her the refrigerator, and she rented the apartment to her friend. Her friend moved out, and she started her day care in the apartment. She asked me if I could do the repairs once she opened it. I agreed to help her with the repairs. She opened the daycare around 2007. I did all the repairs for no money. I paid my carpenter out of my pocket to install the floor. I did not have the money, but I did it from my heart. After six months, she wanted to move out of the apartment into a building. She asked me to give her an estimate for the construction at the new place. I told her for $500, I would remodel the new day care. She said that was too much money. I did not talk to her any more about it. She wanted me to do it for free. She hired another carpenter for the job for over $5,0000, and at the end, he left her. The carpenter did not finish the job. She came running back to me to finish the job she did not want me to do. I forgave her, and I finished the job. Six months after being in a new building, she wanted a bigger space. This time, she did not come to me. She hired the same carpenter for the job. He did not finish the job. She claimed he walked out on her for no reason, and she had no one to finish the job, so she asked me again. I was just trying to help her as a father. After I finished the job, I asked her to make me some macaroni cheese because I was having all my children over at my house. She promised to make it. After a week passed, I was ready to pick up the food on the following Sunday. I called her Sunday morning, and she picked up the phone. She sounded sleepy, and she did not make it because she was up all night. So she asked her aunt to make it. My daughter told me to come get the food, and when I got there, her aunt was pouring milk in a great big pan with no cheese in it. She cooked it in the oven and gave it to me when it finished cooking. Her aunt told me my daughter just gave a party for her ex-boyfriend that she put out for another man. I was highly disappointed with my daughter's action because she told me she had no money to finish the remodeling at the day care. She lied to me. She had money to do the job. She spent money giving a party for her ex-boyfriend. She is just like her mother, conniving and using me for money. I was being used by her because she only called when she wanted me to get her out of a bad situation. I strongly believed she did want to pay those previous carpenters. She wanted to know her father, but she never wanted a relationship with me or her siblings. I took the money out of my pocket. I did not have to pay my carpenter. She had a slick side about her I never knew about when I met her for the first time at twenty-one. This was why my wife wanted me to take the DNA test—to protect me. But I could not see it at the time. I was so deep into being her father I took no time to think what my wife was saying was true. I knew nothing about this girl or her family. What I did learn about the people she was raised by was they were not educated. Most of her relatives did drugs and drink; none had a career, low life. But I continued to ignore my wife's advice. I tried to make something right that was not right. My friend warned me about how she felt about me, and I did not listen to her. I wanted to find out for myself if she was a fake.

Chapter 5

My wife is the wisest woman I've ever been involved with. She could see right through to you. My wife is the strongest person I have ever dated. She may have her ways, but she cannot be moved so easily. She may get emotionally upset with me, but she means no harm. She had her own issues she had to deal with in her life, a father that preferred one daughter over the other daughter. She was emotionally scarred herself, but she managed to survive. So I understood when at times she had to lash out at me for no reason. She has good intentions. She would not have my new daughter that I claimed to be mine without any real proof. We men should listen to our wives when it is to our benefit. I struggled to understand my wife's behavior in the beginning that drove me to be unfaithful. After my last daughter was born, I asked God to help me overcome my unfaithfulness and work on me. I repented from my sins and stayed focused on my wife and children. After finishing up two years of college, I focused on finishing raising our children. It was not easy for me dealing with my adult children and my wife and our children.

What I did was the most important. I always relied on God to lead me and my family. I always stayed committed keeping my children involved with the church. I promised God I would lead them into the path of righteousness. I knew if this marriage was going to work, I needed God all the time. I could not do it by myself. I did accept God at my church. I was coming from the club. I was deeply distressed with myself. I saw my marriage going down the drain, and I needed divine intervention. And that night, I asked God to deliver me from my misery. I was very lonely during those times. I always loved my wife. I knew she was the person for me. God did answer my prayer. I gave my heart to Jesus, so I joined the church again, and my wife was baptized with me. She was pregnant with our second child when we were baptized. We started our Christian journey together as a couple, but it was hard for my wife. She was not accustomed to keeping the Sabbath. I had no problem keeping the Sabbath from my previous marriage. I was more committed to God now than in my past life. I tried working harder to understand God for myself. I wanted to live a Christian life. I did not understand God's purpose for me in my younger days. I was more involved with church activities than in the past. I was a partaker of electing officers for the church, and I volunteered to be a Sabbath schoolteacher and a deacon. I learned more about the Bible being a Sabbath schoolteacher. I was learning my way and understanding the scriptures. I was growing in the scriptures. My parental skills improved, and I did things differently from my older children. I developed more patience being a father and in handling family problems. Mrs. Scott was my mentor. I always consulted her when I had problems with my daughter and children. She had a lot more experience when it came to family matters. She was the only woman in the church I could actually trust. She was a real person; no fake in her. She also trained me to give Bible studies. She was trustworthy.

I kept my distance from other church members. I kept an open mind about people. I never entertained many people at my house. I stayed to myself. My wife and I were secluded; we kept to ourselves. We came from Stamford and moved to Bridgeport. We did not know those people like getting to really know them. There was so much drama in the church. We stayed to ourselves. Some of them thought their children were better than others in the church. I taught my children to be themselves. It was important to me not to compare my children with anyone's child in the church. What I did like about the church was the children always went on trips.

The only time I was mistreated by the leaders was when my daughter had a sweet-sixteen party. The pastor suspended the children and me for the dance at my house, where the head deacon's wife and head elder's wife were dancing with the children. My wife never took part with them, and I was at work. I was very disappointed with the pastor because they just had a party with secular music dancing. I never wanted to teach or be a deacon after the suspension was lifted. The pastor only suspended the children and me because he thought my son wrote his daughter a bad letter when it was another child in the church. I did put the pastor in his place behind closed doors. "I have no problems with you coming after me, but leave my children out of it."

There was so much drama in the church I no longer got involved with leadership. Some of the people were so wicked I changed my membership to another church. I never imagined the church would have so many unconverted Christians. That is the main reason I left thar world, for peace, and I realized not all people in the church are saints. The church members stayed in other people's business. That is why my family stayed to ourselves. My children were broken when they were suspended from their duties. They never took part in any position again. The pastor and most of the leaders were hypocrites. They could dance to secular music, but it was wrong for the children. I did not agree with them. Some of them tried to call my children bad when most of their children were having sex. Some of them were having babies underage. I was deeply hurt by their bad actions. The elder and deacon should have been suspended since their wives were engaged in the party. The pastor and head elder tried to convince me to come back to the church, but the damage was done. I gave them my blessing and told the pastor he was not good at handling people. I witnessed at a meeting when he told a young girl her opinion was not important. The meeting was for the young people, and she was right. I am not the type to agree with a pastor just because he has a title. I did agree with him when it came to preaching a sermon. He did an excellent job preaching sermons and organizing activities for the children, but he was not the most honest pastor. He did not want to pay for work I did at the church and did not pay my brother all the money for laying the carpet.

I went to the new church and started the Sabbath school department for the children. None of the leaders were involved with uniting the children. I brought them together. I forgave my previous pastor and leaders and some church members for attacking my family. I became a stronger leader and learned to control my temper even when I am right. I wanted to leave the church, but the old life had nothing to offer me. So I gave it to God to make me stronger as a leader. God will fight your battles. My grandmother taught me to leave revenge to the Lord. The pastor had the nerve to tell me I would never be a deacon again in his church. He allowed his personal feelings to get in the way of God calling him. It is God's decision if he wants me to have any position in the church, not the pastor's. God is the head of the church and his Son, Jesus. I did become a deacon again and a Sabbath teacher again. In the new church, I organized the Sabbath school and taught the children their lesson every week and was elected deacon again. I always gave my position all that I can give to please God Almighty. This was another sad period of my life, but I conquered all my thoughts that were trying to hold me back. I gained victory over my enemies. God continued to heal my spirit week by week. I was back on track again.

After I completed my task at the church. I went back to my old church to refresh. The elder asked me to teach and be a deacon again. I told him I would give it some thought and get back to him. Weeks later, I did confront him about the position. I tried it again. I left the church and came back again being the only male teacher. The children were out of control again. The female Sabbath schoolteachers could not manage the children. The children had no discipline, along with the pastor's children. I enjoyed teaching the children their lesson. But the female teacher did not want me to teach with her, so she stopped coming to church. She complained that I would let her teach. I was willing to let her teach, but she never came to church. She was cold and lacking kindness. I did not let it stop me from doing God's work. I was always willing to step back. All I cared about is helping people, not concerned about a title. I just wanted to do God's will. I never thought I would experience prejudice in the church. I thought church was a place where Christians love each other through the blood of Jesus. I found out quickly that it was not true. I just wanted to serve the children with my heart. The problem was I was American, and she was Jamaican. She blamed me for not teaching the lesson on Sabbath, but she stopped coming to church which gave me no choice but to look after the well-being of the children. I continued to dedicate myself to those children. Most of them were missing something from their lives. Most of them were being raised by single mothers, and some were raised by grandparents and foster parents. They needed someone to teach them how the Bible relates to the real world. I touched their hearts. Most of them were uncontrollable, and that included the pastor's children. I was not only their Sabbath schoolteacher but a friend. I was struck by the way I disciplined week by week. I helped the uncontrollable children to become tame. They appreciated me more than the other Sabbath schoolteachers who were females. The female Sabbath schoolteachers could not control them. My gift from God was teaching. I gave 100 percent every week. The children loved my style of teaching. I was well connected to them. I was once asked by the superintendent for Sabbath school if I was ever in the army. I told her no. My grandparents and Mother taught us how to behave in church. It stuck to me. I was raised in the South which taught us values and morals. The parents never taught them how to respect their elders. We always addressed adults as Mr. or Mrs. or Ms., but up North, the children had no manners. But I never gave up on the children. I wanted the best for them. Some of the children who grew up as adults always let me know they appreciated me. I felt good inside about their compliments. The children were great to teach. I had no bad experience regarding the children, only the adults. Most of them were Jamaican but were not friendly. They knew their Bibles but did not know how to apply God's scriptures in their lives. I was miserable around those Christians. But after they suspended me for no reason, I never wanted to teach again. But God always has a plan for you. I forgave them for violating me and my family. It took me a while to get over this situation, but I did bounce back at the new church. I realized not all Christians are honest and faithful. I never experienced this discourse in my previous churches; most of them were cold as ice. I got so depressed I spoke before church.

That Sabbath morning, I interrupted the morning program by expressing my feelings about how cold people's hearts were inside their bodies. They were unloving Christian adults. The children had all the love. I left after I spoke my mind. I was actually sad about coming to that church. This was the first time in twenty years I witnessed an unconverted Christian. Some of them called me demon possessed, and others said I was truly a man of God. I continued going there with my family for a year, and then I had my family membership moved to another church. I not only had drama at home but also in the church. I was happy that I always stayed to myself. I was not trying to get close to anyone in the church because I did not want my wife and I to get too personal with them.

I never trusted anyone because of the things done to my daughters. After a couple of bad divorces, I was guarding my feelings against future attacks. My first wife spent ten years attacking me and my second wife with child abuse. It was sad because she did not want the marriage to work. She did all things to make my second wife unhappy by dragging her to court. This tore her apart mentally, causing her to use drugs to overcome the pain. She was an excellent stepmother and good wife until she lost control of her life. The drugs became her life. It is a good thing we ended the marriage as friends. I found love again with my third wife. I didn't plan it this way. It just happened that way. I would have loved to follow God's original plan of marrying, only having one wife. But it takes two to tango, not one. True love is between people in love with each other to survive. My wife now was looking for the love that could last forever.

My first was so jealous of my new happiness she started again about child abuse that never happened. But this time, she left my wife out of the complaint and dragged me to court again, but I became my own lawyer in court. I learned from my lawyer how to file legal documents to avoid wasting money I could use for my family. The cases were always dismissed by the court. The court was familiar with her lies by now. My wife stayed her distance from my ex-wife. I decided to file for child support since she had so much time trying to destroy me and my marriage. Months later, the case came before a judge and awarded me forty-five per child. I had two daughters by her. She stayed out of my business after she had to pay child support every week. I waited for the child support to add up to five thousand, and I used that as leverage to keep her out of my business. She tried on one occasion to come into my house without my consent. I never wanted her inside my house anymore. She tried to force herself in my house while my wife was upstairs, and we got into a fight. We both got scars from the fight, and she called the police to arrest me, but nothing happened. The police gave us both summons to come to court. We went to family court, and a year later, the case was dismissed. She went back to her mother's house and lied to our youngest daughter that I beat her up, but she never told her she tried to force herself into my apartment, and she attacked me. She initiated the fight. My wife and I continued to live in harmony with my daughters. It was never easy for me to raise my daughters. Their mother always tried to stir up trouble when she could. She never came over to my house again with her boyfriends to pick fights with my wife and me. She was afraid of my wife. She stayed clear of her. After our daughter had a baby, she backed off for a couple of years. Now she wanted a favor from me. The court was going to arrest her for back child support, and she wanted me to sign a waiver to get off the hook. She promised if I signed a waiver for her not to pay the back money, she would pay me, but she never did pay me. I did not care about the money. I signed the waiver. It did not make sense to see her locked up in jail. My daughter needed her mother to help her raise my granddaughter.

My wife and I both worked on our jobs every week. I always provided for all my wives. My first wife never worked during the time we lived together as husband and wife. It was their choice to work. I was focused on building up J.R. Home Improvement. I was delivering papers at night and working my business in the daytime. I was able to put myself through college. I graduated in two years, and my wife and children along with other family members celebrated my success at a restaurant. I made bad choices, not protecting myself regarding sex. I got my high school girlfriend pregnant that prevented me from going to college. It was a setback for me, but I chose to be a father. I never regretted delaying college. I never gave up the dreams of getting my degree. Sometimes, being young, you make bad decisions, but at some point, you will grow from them. I told my guidance counselor I wanted to achieve two things in my life: finish college and go into my own business. After I married my third wife, I did both and later bought my own house. I did not let my daughter stop me from dreaming. I wanted more out of life. I kept pushing forward toward my goals. I did not have my wife's support when starting my new business. She did not have faith in me. She wanted me to stay on a job. I was not satisfied with making a little money on a job. She was comfortable working for other people; that wasn't for me. I wanted to grow mentally and financially. I was already growing spiritually. I struggled without her support. It just made me stronger and stronger. I was never a man to let anyone convince me what I could not do. In this book on how to be positive by Napoleon Hill, it says that if you can conceive it, believe it, then you can certainly achieve it. It was embedded in my thoughts. There was nothing my wife could say to change my mind. That was one of the things I did not like about. She never had any dreams. I was disappointed in her not giving me any support, but I proved her wrong. I made enough money to put myself through two years of college, and I did not owe the college any money when I graduated.

My wife is a great mother and dedicated employee. The children always had a cooked meal. She always went to church with me. I was always stronger than her spirit. I was the one who made sure my children went to church. My wife was not an outdoor person, so I took the children to the park and their doctor's appointments. I never forced God on her. When I started college, she was not that supportive of me going back to school. She felt it was a waste of time, but I never looked at it that way. Sometimes wives can be jealous of their husbands' success. She never finished two years of college, but she did do one year. That could have been the reason why she did not want me to go to college, because she never succeeded. I was told by her parents she graduated, but years later, it was a lie. But I did not hold that against her. She had a good heart. It took me years to realize she meant well. She cared in a different way. She never told me she graduated from college. I believed her parents, but I found out later it was a lie when she came home crying. She was always sensitive. She lost a job because she stated she graduated, and she did not complete two years of college. I gave her my support and told her not to worry about it. My wife was very sensitive and emotional about losing her job. I was not worrying about the money. My wife loves working and found another job. We had our ups and downs, but we never gave up on our marriage. We remained solid. We always made up after any disagreement. We always had great sex. Most people do not want to talk about how great sex is in their relationship, but it is part of marriage.

I continued to work hard in my business, and after three years, I did not need a job anymore I was making money. I had four work vehicles with my company name on it. I was able to buy a second house and work toward my bachelor's degree, which I plan to finish in the near future. I never gave up on my dreams to finish college and start my own business. I never imagined that my ex-wife would be nonproductive in her designing career and would be so vicious. After she had an affair with her coworker, she went downhill in her career. Afterward, I worked so hard to make sure she finished high school because she was sixteen years old when we married and pushed her through designing school when she wanted to give up on school. I stuck by her, but our plan was for her to finish first, and then I would go back to college once she completed trade school. She could design like the top designers, but she took the wrong path. After I gave all those professional fashion shows to boost her career, it all went nowhere. She did not take the advantage going forward in her career. All the talent God gave her went to waste. I continued to grow financially and mentally. I was determined to be successful in business and attain a higher education. I was not giving up at any cost.

When I met my third wife, all my past failures became a success. I went back into business the third time after my last two business ventures failed. I cried like a baby because I wanted it so bad. It really hurt, but I never gave up hope. In my first business, I learned to be a salesman and connect with other businesspeople, and in the fashion world, I learned to organize people and market my business. So when I started my home improvement business, I combined those skills from my previous business. And taking my first business course in college gave me the edge to be successful. My professor gave me a piece of knowledge that opened my mind to success. I knew from failing the first two times I lacked money to succeed. I figured it out later. So when I started my new business, I delivered paper at night and worked my business in the morning. My first two carpenters were not good for me, so I connected with two experienced carpenters to advance to the next level. They both took me under their wings to teach me the trade. After five years working under the best, I became a skilled worker. My carpenters advised me to learn the business to protect my business. They advised me correctly because at times, I had to finish most of my jobs myself. They taught me how to read blueprints, so when I went to college, my grade after the semester was a B. It made the course easier for me. I knew I needed more education to move forward in business. My wife could not understand why it was so important to continue my education. College was making me wiser and helping me to stay more focused on my goals. Man without a dream is dead. If you don't have a dream, you're dead; you are not living. In order to be happy with oneself, you must dream.

I grew in my business and maintained a stable marriage. My ex-wife interfered with our progress in our marriage and interfered with the second marriage with her vicious attacks. She wasted her time trying to destroy me, but actually, she was destroying herself. I knew what I wanted in life: to be successful in business and find a wife to be happy. I found my wife, and she was the one to help further my goals. We had our struggles the first five years, but we managed to stay focused. We did not agree on business, but we had the same common goals on raising our children. We wanted the best for them. No matter what our situation was at the time, we always made up by the end of the night. We both worked hard to maintain a healthy relationship. It is a shame she spent all the years being hateful when she could have used the energy to advance her career. I never expected her to be like that at all because in high school, she always talked about the Bible and during the marriage while living together, until she failed from grace and never regained her stature. After our daughters turned eighteen, she backed off from attacking me because she could not use them as pawns. She became another person after the separation. She never came back to herself again. She continued to be with more than one man sexually; that was her new addiction. All I wanted was to be with only one woman, so I asked God to deliver me from the lust of the flesh.

I have been faithful to my current wife. My family is the most important part of my life. Most of our minor troubles were dealing with our children growing into their teenage years. France's problem was boys, and I had to protect her from getting pregnant. It was my biggest concern, making sure they graduated before being a parent and hoping they would go to college. That was my only fear: my daughters having babies or my son. I never compared my children to other people's children. They are mine. I wanted them to do their best. My son, Riggie, is smart and friendly. No matter where we went, people grasped to him. He wins your heart. But the only problem I had with him was he was caught walking out the store with an earring in his left ear. He was arrested, and I went to the police station to get him. We went to court a few times and the case was dropped and it was closed. The adviser gave my son some wise counsel. "You have a concerned father. It is not worth getting in trouble." I had no more problems with him. Cookie was a boy crazy, but she made it through high school. The only trouble I had with her was when she went to the mall with her niece, and her niece got caught stealing. They were taken to the police station. I had to come get her. She never went to court. I had no problem with her. Rachel was caught stealing and she went to the police station and me and my wife went to get her. She went to counseling for six months, and the charges were dismissed. They all finished high school, and some went to college and started their own business. I had a little trouble in their teenage years. They were good children. I kept them in church every Sabbath, and the church had plenty of activities for the children every week. I spent time with them spiritually. I made sure they were taught the Bible and taught them how to pray. My wife was not grounded like me, but we all went to church together. It was important that God's Word was the foundation for my family. I made a promise to God that if he gave me a second chance to serve him, I would bring them up in the Word. I stuck to my promise, and I made sure I was the priest in my family. It was not easy at times because my wife was not participating in family worship with us. I had to do it alone until they grew up.

Another chapter started in our life. My daughter was now expecting a baby. In her last year of high school, we found out from a church sister that our daughter was pregnant. I was not angry because I already experienced it with her oldest sister. We gave her all our support. It seemed church members put their children out of the house, and some of them were making their children get abortion. We were doing neither one of those things. We love our children. We made sure she took full responsibility for her baby. After she had her baby, she got her a job. Frances had the baby in June; she graduated the same month. She got a job right away. My son had his first child at twenty-three, and he moved out of my house into his own apartment with his girlfriend. He became a responsible young man. He decided to go to college and go into his own business. He learned business at thirteen when I took him to the construction site. My carpenter was training him. I never had to buy his clothes because he worked every summer. I was grooming him to be a good husband for the right woman. My son provides for his family. He is dedicated to his family. Cookie graduated from high school. Now she got pregnant a year after having her first child. She stayed home. She moved out a year later into her apartment. She always had a job after graduation. A year later, she moved back into our house. We rented her the third-floor apartment.

I have some beautiful grandchildren, and all of them are well-mannered. I am proud of my six children being responsible adults. Their oldest sisters finished four years of college. When it came to God and getting an education, I made it clear it is important to be grounded. Rachel is my baby daughter. She is the wisest of all of them. She does not want any children. She is focused on business. She learned what not to do from her siblings. I learned what not to do from my oldest brothers. I did not want the fast life of many girlfriends and too many babies all over the place. I wanted to be in the same house raising my children. God allowed me to raise them together as sisters and only one brother. God made it possible for me to be grounded as a family man. No matter what takes place with my children, they know how to forgive each other. Rachel tried college, but she preferred being in her own business. She is grounded in business. My son and I taught her business at a young age. She was about sixteen when exposed to business. I exposed all of them to business at an early age. I always encouraged them to do what makes them happy career wise. My dreams are not their dreams. They have to find their own dreams. I will always support their dreams 100 percent. Every man and woman has to find their own path to life, not someone else's path. If you keep doing what you want, it will eventually happen. You should never give up even if it seems impossible. There were times when I wanted to give up on marriage and finishing college, but I kept craving success. If you do not try, how would you know if you could succeed? I kept pushing for a better marriage, better business, and to attain a bachelor's degree against all odds. Success comes by not giving up. There is a song we sing in church, "Victory Is Mine." Victory is for all of us who want it. It is not about the person that started the race but the person that finished the race. I made it across the finish line many times. I did get my associate degree and bachelor's degree. I did my business work. I did buy some houses in my lifetime. I remained married for thirty-six years. I have achieved all my goals that I want to accomplish. I am truly happy about life. My last goal was to write this book that I was working on each and every day. I am still setting new goals for my life because I want to continue growing until God takes me from this life. I want to continue being an inspiration to my family and others to do better. I still want to make a difference in society and the world. In order to make a difference, you must show the world you can make a difference to others. I have inspired my friend Charlie for over thirty-five years to be better. He has known all my wives. He knows me better than my biological brothers. We share feelings and thoughts about life situations all the time.

Love is confusing. You do not know what to expect from it. In my early life, I knew nothing about love. I learned a great deal from my first girlfriend. She was compassionate and full of zeal. After breaking her heart, she broke my heart. I found the true meaning of love. Love is not supposed to hurt at all; love is supposed to be joyful. I was never taught to love nor the meaning of love. Love is so deep most people do not understand the true meaning of love. It is something that comes and goes, but it is real when you understand it. It is two hearts blended together. But sometimes, two hearts never blend together. Sometimes it is not balanced, causing pain. This is what makes it confusing not being equally yoked. Love is a good feeling when it is equally balanced. Love is the greatest feeling God input in man and woman. Adam and Eve had the perfect love until sin entered the human race.

I do not know if human beings can experience the true meaning of love. Love is deeper than the eyes can see. I am still trying to find the true balance of love. Love can disappear under your eyes if you are not careful. After I lost my first wife, I started searching for the true meaning of love. After I found my second wife, I was beginning to understand love. But she never stayed around enough for love to blossom. People love for the wrong reasons, for money or maybe sex. People love things more than people, so they never get the chance to experience true love. Sometimes love walks out the door underneath your eyes. Love is often taken for granted. Love never stays the same all the time. Sometimes love is up and sometimes down. It is complicated most of the time. I am so perplexed about love. It seems harder to understand it. When I think I am getting closer to love, it drops again like a thermostat. Love is the most challenging feeling on earth.

My father never knew the true meaning of love between a woman and man. It was impossible for him to pass down the true meaning of love to his offspring. My mother was confused about true love because my father never showed her love. Now I am left to find the true meaning of love from God. It was hard to give any woman the true meaning of love if I never saw it. I began to learn about the true meaning of love from my heavenly Father through the Scriptures. I never experienced my mother and father embracing their love, leaving me lacking the true meaning of love. I never experienced the hugging and kissing because love did not last long. I began to grasp the meaning of love after a few broken loves.

When I met my last wife, I knew the true meaning of love. I was willing to give it all at all cost. I was full of love and passion. I was not the same person I used to be, lacking the understanding of love. My wife's love is confusing because she does not understand the true meaning of love. She never experienced true love because of her father showing lack of love to his wife. Now I have to work harder to maintain her love. She is the most confusing person I have ever met in my life. I have to bring out the love in her. She is sometimes up with her love and sometimes down. She was like me, never knowing the true meaning of love, love being misinterpreted. I am deeply troubled regarding her love because her love is hidden and has to be brought to the surface. She is the most confusing person I have met in my life. She is different from the others. She was troubled from the love her father never gave, leaving her stuck, preventing her from true love. She has a clue how to love, but the past feeling is holding her back. She has the wrong concept of love, and she is trying to figure it out. We both are trying to hold onto love. We both have to balance our love to make it last. Love cannot last unless we both find a balance. If there is no balance, love will fade away slowly. Love does hurt when you are trying your hardest to keep it alive. Love is deeper than the eyes can see but mostly misunderstood. It takes time for two hearts to blend; it takes years of work. Love can only exist if love is interpreted the right way. True love is not controlling each other but trusting each other, making the right decision for each other. In order for love to work, we have to think about why we fail at love. Love is a lifetime commitment, always being considerate about each other's feelings. With true love, you always find time to forgive each other's faults. True love is having God work it out for you. Love is difficult at times, but it can work if two blend their thoughts into one thought. I love both parties.

My oldest brother and sister never cultivated the true meaning of love for me because they were never taught love and forgiveness toward others. They both are the same people inside who hold grudges for life. My sister and brother are still worried about a car that broke down thirty-five years ago. It was never my fault. My sister and brother never stepped foot in my house. My children do not know too much about them being their aunt and uncle. My brother stayed angry at my stepmother until she died because she would not sell him my grandfather's car. He never visited her until he went to her funeral. My sister is still angry at my mother because she was not raised by my mother. They both are still angry and bitter. They do not know the true meaning of love. I knew she never knew about me like the rest of the siblings, but I forgave her anyway because my grandmother taught me not to hold onto grudges, to let God work out your salvation. I visited my sister all the time at her house, but she never came to mine when I invited her. But she told me she loves me. This is misinterpreted love because she does not give me equal love like her other siblings. She has fake love, but my oldest hates it for no reason. He was not taught true love because his father never showed true love to our mother. All my brother's life, he has used and abused all his girlfriends and wife. My father never taught him how to treat a woman or to be a man. I have gone to him many times to make peace, and last time, my wife and mother witnessed that I was trying to give him love. He pretended he loved me in front of my mother, giving me a fake hug. He fooled my mother, but he did not fool me. He went to my daughters telling them he still holds a grudge. He has walked by me many times at funerals and family functions and would not say a word to me but hugged my wife and daughter. He never forgave me for something that was not my fault. He lent me a car that broke down on the New Jersey turnpike. My father paid to fix it, and he wanted me to pay him again. He always was crooked. I would have never done that to him. My sister lent me a car forty-five years ago knowing I could not drive a car with a clutch. I burned the clutch out, but I offered her money to fix the clutch. She did not want me to help fix the car.

Most of my siblings did bad things to me, but I never held a grudge against them. My next-oldest brother wrecked my Lincoln being drunk, but I was not mad at him. I reported it to my insurance company, and the insurance company fixed the car. What was important to me was that he did not get hurt. We are still close today. My youngest brother damaged my garage on purpose, but I never held a grudge against him. I love him anyway. I forgave him. Most of them are jealous because I lived a Christian life and raised all my children. I have a solid marriage. Most of my siblings were like our father. They never respected their wives, and my sister never picked the right husband. Her husband left her. She is still bitter like my other sisters. They were not faithful to their husbands. They had problems because I made my marriage work. I never stopped loving my wife, and I tried my hardest to be faithful. My children had a chance to experience the true meaning of love. I took the time to teach them the true purpose of love. I took the time to teach my son how to be a man and how to be a loving father. I taught my daughters, "Never settle for less if a man is not going to put a ring on your finger. Do not let them move into your apartment. You have a better chance at getting someone productive and respectful."

In my lifetime, so many people disrespected me, but I always forgave people. I let God fight my battles for me. When I helped my daughter, I claimed her at twenty-one. I never hated her for using me. I forgave her for what she did to me. I knew the day I met her she was not like my children I raised with my current wife. I knew there was never gonna be a true bond between us because of a lie her mother told her. She never knew love. She grew up with a man who never loved her mother and had an abusive boyfriend. All the twenty-one years, I knew she lived with different men that did not love her. I tried to instill some values in her, but she had those immoral ways like her mother. She was skilled in manipulating others in her surroundings. I tried to show genuine love to her, but she still had grudges against me from childhood. I did not know she existed, and her mother was not looking for me. I found out twenty-one years later. Even though I did not take a DNA test, I stepped in as a father to her. I never felt a real connection of love with her, and she never made me feel like a father and grandfather. The children never call me grandfather at all, only when money was involved in the conversation about how she raised them. The mother passed down a lie to her daughter, and she passed it down to her children. There is no way I can compete with a lie.

When I met her, I cosigned for her first brand-new car. I bought the house she lives in with her children, and I was still not acknowledged as their grandfather. I worked at both day care centers without pay and worked on her garage roof that was falling apart. I never got paid for the work. After she established herself years later, she opened a second day care. This time she was about to lose the house and business because the contractor underbid the work. She begged me to do the job. She had no money to pay me what the job was worth. I did it, but I did not make any money from my craftsmanship. It was rough on me because I had to do all the work by myself. I could not hire qualified help, so I abused my body overworking. She was a nasty person to work for, and I began to see she had a grudge against me. She spoke to me in a negative way. She was rudely texting me. She was very disrespectful. She did not treat me like her father. She was completely different when I met her at twenty-one years ago. I was getting frustrated about the job. I wanted to walk away from it. But she refused to pay me. I had no energy to remain working for her. She was a complete stranger to me. I packed my tools and equipment and never came back. I went to her house to get my money to pay my helper. She refused to pay me. I brought a witness with me. She accused me of being a thief in front of her new boyfriend, friend, and children. I told her to keep the money and went toward the door to leave. She stood up in front of all those people telling lies. I never did anything and got out of the house I bought. She had her friends and family think she accomplished financial success by herself. I was mad and made a comment that I never took a DNA test. So she had her uncle threaten me. I reported him to the police. The police officer contacted her uncle by phone and spoke to him. If he threatened me again, he would be arrested. She lied to her uncle that she paid me.

Now I see what my wife has been saying for years. "She only wants you for money and things you can do for her." I knew my wife was correct all these years. I tried to protect her, but she was doing the opposite. I was deeply saddened by her, but I forgave her. I still love her, but I kept my distance after she called the police the next day to have me arrested. I got past the hurts, and I never looked back. I tried to show kindness toward her children by giving them Christmas gifts every year, but they were ungrateful like their mother. They never called me at all thanking me for the gifts. This is another case of love misinterpreted. She never knew true love because her mother lived with a man without being married. She had a nasty side about her I never knew. She is still a bitter person. God gave me the spirit of forgiveness. I reached out to her, and she never tried to discuss how to mend the relationship. It's been seven years since she spoke to me, but I overcame her. I had my family troubles, but it never allowed me to be bitter. I love my enemies and those who despise me. God had given me the victory over all my enemies. What happened in my life with my family and church family have made me a stronger and better human being. I refused to let anyone take my happiness from me. I love God too much to hate anyone. My oldest brother and sister could never be blessed spiritually or mentally because they do not know God like me. I am a survivalist. My faith is stronger than ever. I have always been a fighter. I will fight for happiness for the rest of my life.

My wife always could see through people. She is a good judge of character. Only God can give you perfect peace, and I rely on God for perfect peace. My children are taught to rely on God for peace and protection. I pray for Nireen and others in my family who hate. My wife is the strongest woman I have ever been out of all my past relationships. We do not let our disagreements get in the way of our love. We have forgiven each other for over thirty-six years. Our love is much stronger than the day we met. We are learning to appreciate each other every year. We both have our faults, but we never let it get in our way of loving each other. We had family on both sides to cause confusion, but we overcame all the negative vibes. We overcame the headaches and pain. We respected each other more as time passed. We understand love more and more, and it gets deeper and deeper. The only way we can mend our hearts is through forgiveness, God's way. We show our children true love between a man and a woman. We are not afraid to embrace our love for each other. Our love is so deep nothing can get between it. Love is giving it all to the person and not withholding it.

Chapter 6

Love can be misinterpreted by people you love. My father never treated me like the rest of his children. He treated me with less kindness. I watched him give all my siblings money, and he never would give me money when I asked him. My father attacked me when I was younger for no reason. I pretended to run away to my friend's apartment upstairs. I came back later that night, and he apologized to me. I never had that close relationship with my father growing up. As I grew into adulthood, I moved away from the relationship. My father never had any good advice on how to treat a woman. He was too busy having sex with all the ladies in the neighborhood. My two oldest brothers were having sex with the women's daughters. My two brothers impregnated their daughters while living with their wives. He was not a true example as a father. In my early years, I never wanted to follow his path. I clung to my mother because she made sure I learned morals. She always had her friends take us to church. When I married my first wife, I stayed away from my father and siblings. My father was dishonest to me. He paid to fix my car to have peace with my brother. This was misinterpreted love. My father kept my brand-new car with my brother. I called the police on my brother to have my car returned to me. My father and brother were scheming all the time against me. It took years to figure out that my father was on my oldest brother's side. I lost respect from my father when he told me he would have sex with my second wife. I love him because my mother instilled love in me. My father took my money when I worked all summer and gave it to my baby brother. He promised to give my money back to me. He never gave me my money. I will never forget it. I remember I asked him for some money, but he said he did not have any money. He pulled a roll of money before my eyes. He never treated me and my brothers and sister equal. He always gave them money when they asked him. He never discussed the Bible or prayed with me. He was worldly.

After we moved to Connecticut, he tried to fight my mother, but this time, she cut him with a knife. The reason why my brothers stole and chased women is because my father was a bad role model. My oldest brother was trifling like my father. He did not care whom he had sex with at all. He had a baby by his ex-girlfriend and slept with her daughter and had a baby by the girl he helped raise. And my brother's oldest son molested his first cousin when he had a wife at home. They do not care whom they hurt. I was deeply saddened that my nephew did that to me. I was the one who got him a job when he came up north. I was the uncle that told his wife not to leave him. I could never trust any of them alone with my children or grandchildren. This is love misinterpreted. My oldest brother has always been crooked. I gave him $700 to buy me a car. I was seventeen at the time. He never bought me the car. I had to gamble with his friends to get my money. I lost the money in a card game. I will never gamble with him again. But he was cursed. He had four stores, but he gambled all his money away, and he did not profit at all. He lost all the stores because of a bad gambling habit, another bad habit he got from my father and my next-to-oldest brother.

My sister, raised by my grandmother, was never taught by my father on how to find a good husband. My sister hated her baby's father because he raped her. She was only fifteen, and he was twenty. She tried to control every man she went with and married. She is the most miserable person in the family. They all broke off the relationship. She smothered her men to the point they would never come back. She served them in bed and brought them slippers. They loved it for a time but moved on with their lives.

My oldest brother is the worst out of my father's ten children. It was his way or the highway. He was spoiled rotten by my parents. All my siblings ate him up except me. I was an independence thinker. He was jealous of my good nature. My character was like my mother. My mother was thoughtful of others, and my father cared less whom he hurt My brother was like my father, treacherous and reckless. He has been jealous of me since I became an adult. I was eighteen when he told me he was going to be a millionaire before me. I never thought about being a millionaire. All I wanted in life was to be a caring father and be able to take care of my children financially. I wanted to live a Christian life. It got to the point he wanted to kill me because I was not like him. I remember he lent me his car to go to work and transport my children to school and the babysitter. He charged me for using the car before I lent him money. He took the car, and I was left walking everywhere with my daughters. I worked in his stores faithfully and never took any money from him. He accused me of stealing, and I stopped working for him. He was not kind to me, and the rest of my years, he never cared about me. He could not control me like the other siblings. He had a habit of telling his friends I was not his brother. My grandmother told me before she died that one day, when he would be coming down, I would be moving up in life. After he lost all his stores from gambling, he was going downhill. I was moving up the ladder with my business, education, and a stable family life. I had the luxury to raise my six children in my house and support another that I do not know if she's mine. He never had that luxury to raise his children in his household. He was never stable, like my father. One of his children's mothers did not want his name on the birth certificate in order not to pay child support. He never paid support to that girl child. His oldest son has the same characteristics of his father. His other son is honest. My brother's jealousy against me was so deep that my mother told me to never trust him. He never lived a morally good life. He did not have the capability to teach good because his heart spiritually was bad. I pray that he gets it right before he dies.

What my grandmother told me in my twenties came to light. After the age forty, I was beginning to understand what my grandmother was telling me. I began to prosper, and morally, I was a better man than him. I never used people because I did not want to be used by people. My brother used everyone that came into his path, but in the end, he came out bitter to the point he does not associate with his own children. He does not have those characteristics as a father and grandfather. He made over $100,000, and God never blessed his money. He gambled it all away. Now he is broke. And he is still mentally abusing his new wife. He controls his wife like a child. Now he has ran out of options and that left her the only person to control. This is love misinterpreted.

My nextoldest brother followed his path. He is a follower, not a leader. He is still falling in the hand of my oldest brother. Whenever my oldest brother wants money, he calls my brother to gamble with his friends. My next-oldest brother works hard for his money and makes more than my oldest brother. He makes over $125,000 a year. I hate when they gamble because sometimes a fight breaks out because someone is cheating. I almost got cut one time trying to break them up from fighting, but my older brother was cut by a knife by our brother. My oldest brother stayed in the hospital for weeks. The next time I tried to stop them from fighting, I had to use a karate kick on him. After I kicked him, I went to my car and pulled off. My sister grabbed my car door trying to help my oldest brother. She was dragged a little. And my brother would have been run over if he did not move himself from the front of my car. After that incident, I never went around them for years. They had too much drama. They were not happy unless they had some type of drama in their lives. My next-oldest brother was always kind to me. We always had a good relationship, but he had his flaws also. As the years went by, a little jealousy sprouted up but not of hate. He felt bad that with all the money he made, I was doing better than him financially. He became similar to my oldest brother who wanted to outdo me. He never allowed himself to be bitter against my success. He was happy for me but regretted that he made a bad decision in his lifetime. My oldest brother wanted to fight me many times, but this brother stepped in to my rescue. Years ago, when I bought my grandfather's land, he was bitter but not to the point that he wanted to hurt me. I let him know he was jealous of me by stating I came down south to look for a woman. I was not the same person. I matured in time. He did not greet me well that day. He hugged the person that was next to me, but he did not hug me. The rest of the weekend, we got along well. My brother wasted his money on cars and females. He never took the advantage of making his money work for him. He bragged a lot how he made more money than anyone in the family, but at the age of seventy, he does not own a house. My two brothers could have been millionaires if they invested their money in real estate. Not so different with women, my father did not take the time to teach them the value of money when they were growing up as children.

My oldest brother married four times but never settled with the last three wives. He had ten children but started being a father to the last two by his girlfriend that he was with before he married the second and third wife. After the third wife, he finally married his children's mother. She is his fourth wife. Now he is settled a little. He is trying to go to church to do better. He stepped up to the plate to help the oldest children. He taught all his sons and grandchildren a trade. His sons live like him, cars and women but no house with the money they make each year. All his daughters have been to college and graduated. They had great mothers. He still feels bad that I made little money but invested it wisely and have been married to my wife for thirty-six years. He did come to my graduation party with his wife. His wife is a down-to-earth sister-in-law. I told him this about his wife, but he could not see it. She stuck by him when his last two wives walk away from the marriage. His first wife raised his three children without his full support. Love misinterprets again. The last conversation he had with me was talking about all the money in the bank. He wanted to buy a house for cash. No one does that at seventy years old. He was trying to impress me, but I knew he felt jealous of my success. His heart means well. He is nothing but my oldest brother, selfish. It does not hurt me that my oldest doesn't like me. I love and value myself. I am the first and last out of my siblings with a bachelor's degree in management. My sister tried to go to college but never made out the first year, and my half-sister never completed two years of college.

My half-sister is another bitter person, Christie. I met her when I was about thirty years old. My second wife was friendly with her. My sister loves her because she did drugs. I thought she and I were on track with our relationship. After the marriage broke up, my sister became distant after I met my third wife. I realized we were never close. She was close to my youngest brother because he did drugs like her. She came to Connecticut all the time to see my sister and brother, but she never gave me a phone call to visit. My wife and I did not do drugs. We went to church with our children. Last time she came to my house, she acted like she did not want to be there. She came with a friend and wanted to leave. My sister's friend was enjoying herself. My sister had an attitude with my daughter. She had so many bad relationships with her boyfriends. She never had any children because she aborted them. She married her husband but still had the habit of cheating on him. She was just like my father, not faithful. All my father's children inherited those traits. My two sisters both had bad attitudes; that's why they never got along. My half-sister was always competing for my father's love. They would get mad for simple things and would not speak for years. My oldest sister stayed mad at her for about twenty years. They could not be in the same room together. When they did make up, they were mad again because my other half-sister came close to Christie, and all three were competing for my father's love.

My half-sister Betty was trying to get as much money from my father because he gave her up for adoption to her mother's husband. Betty already had resentment against my father because he did not want to support her and her brothers financially, so my father passed the bulk. The only family he supported financially was his ex-wife. The state took out his child support payment every week. My father was still having an affair with Betty's mother while she was still with her husband. I witnessed the phone call when Mrs. Marie asked him to send money and to meet him when he arrived in Virginia. She was cheating with my father while he's married to my mother. Now years later, she was cheating on her husband. My father and he mother cared about no one but themselves. My father never learned to respect himself and other relationships. Now Betty's mother and adopted father are deceased. Betty is only concerned about getting his money. Betty called me one evening talking about how we can get his money when my niece is taking care of my father. I told her I do not need any money from my father and do not care whom he leaves his money to. My half brother Roger, who is Betty's brother from their mother, wants no part of his money. Duke, Roger, and Betty are my father's outside children from Mrs. Marie. Roger and Duke are easy to get along with as brothers because they are not biased. Betty is not so easy to get along with these days. I try to keep my distance from her and my other sisters. They all are miserable people. They are all drama queens. My brothers are much easier to deal with in a relationship. I try to stay away from all the family drama that is why I am happy I live in Connecticut. My father could not get his children to get along with each other because he did not know how to maintain a stable relationship with any of the mothers. The only time my siblings are in agreement is when it comes to me because I am nothing like them.

Sometimes when you think you know people, you do not know them. I knew my wife's sister long before I knew her. One night, I decided to go out to a bar. I left my Cutlass Supreme at home. I walked across town to get some air. I went inside the bar once I arrived. I did not drink, but I just went in to listen to some music. I met my wife for the second time. The first time I met her was a year ago to try out for a fashion show. After the night was over, I was going to walk back to my sister's house. My wife at that time was not my girlfriend. She was coming out of the club, and I asked her for a ride home. I was single again. She gave me a ride to my sister's house. I was visiting my sister with my two daughters. I was living in New York at the time. I asked her for her phone number, and she gave it to me. I called her on the phone regularly. I asked her to be my girlfriend, and we continued seeing each other week after week and month after month. I told her I was going to buy her a house one day, and she laughed on the phone. We enjoyed each other's company. We had great sex. I invited her to my place in New York to cook her dinner. I baked chicken, corn, and mashed potatoes and bought a bottle of wine. When she drove and was close to my house, I met her at the corner, and she followed me to my house. I forgot to turn the oven down low, so when we stepped inside the house, the chicken was burnt. We ate corn and potatoes, drank some wine, and listened to Freddie Jackson album. It was love music, and by the end of the night, we engaged in sex. We continued to see each other all the time. I moved out of New York back to Connecticut into my sister's apartment. I introduced her to my sister. The only word from my sister to me was my girlfriend and I were not going to make it.

I decided to apply for an apartment from the housing authority. I had a friend that works for the office, and she moved my application up for me to get an apartment. It is not how much you know but whom you know that will further your agenda. I moved into my new apartment with my daughters, and later, my girlfriend moved into my apartment. After a few months, she was pregnant with our first daughter. I did not believe in living with anyone unless we were married. I asked her to marry me. I invited my family and her family to be witnesses at my apartment. We married at my apartment, and the only people who came were my wife's mother and my brother and his wife. After six months, our daughter was born. We both struggle mentally getting to know each other as husband and wife. It was new to my wife to have stepchildren to raise, but we stayed focused. It was not easy for us, but we managed to survive.

I was not a Christian when I got married, so I did worldly things. I went to bars every week, and I knew my wife did not like it. We did not visit her sister a lot. She had three children when I met her and her husband. I was not close to them. I had always been too busy working. I had too many responsibilities to mingle with her family and my family. As the years passed, my wife and I had three more children. When the children started going to school, we had to go school shopping. We invited her sister every year to go shopping in New York. We never missed a year. My brother-in-law never went shopping. He had a drinking problem and was not that involved. We took her sister shopping until all children were grown. I thought after all these years, her sister cared about me, but I found out from her daughter's boyfriend that she talked down to me. When she and her husband could not pay their rent, they borrowed from us. My brother-in-law borrowed my money and did not offer to pay me back. He went on his vacation with his wife and played his numbers but never would call me to pay me back. I had to ask for my money back. I do not know if he ever paid my wife back her money. People borrowed money, but they do not want to pay it back. That is the reason I do not like loaning money. I lent my worker some money, and he never paid it back. After loaning my sister-in-law money, she told her daughter's boyfriend I took her sister away from her. She was already married with three children and a husband. She was against me marrying her sister, and I thought I was better than her and her husband. I never displayed that attitude toward anyone. I wanted to be a businessman and attained a college degree. I chose to buy a house for my wife and I wanted something better for my family. All her husband wanted was to stay drunk. He was a good man and father, but she was not a kind person as a wife. She was nasty like her father, a bitter person. He went through hell in that marriage. Their sons never matured as men. She still treats them like babies. Their father never stayed sober to train them to be men. I went through so much mental abuse with my wife's family. I am happy that I was never broken in spirit. My father-in-law was bad news, and my wife's twin brother was just as bad as his sister. I remembered loaning him money for child support to keep him out of jail. My youngest was mad at me and told me her uncle did not like me. I never did anything to him. They all were jealous of me because I was a go-getter. When I set my mind to do something worthwhile I achieved it. I wanted my own business, and I made it work after going through my trial and tribulation. I reinvested in my education and later invested in property. All I wanted to do was give my family a better life. I was never trying to outdo anyone but trying to move forward in life.

My wife was like her family who had no ambition. I did not let her attitude or her family's negativity get in my way of progressing. I raised my six children never to give up on their dreams and that hard work pays off. My oldest finished college with a bachelor's degree, my next to oldest with two master's degrees. I instilled those values in them, to educate themselves, and to the next four, I gave them the same values. They all are productive citizens. My son and baby daughters are entrepreneurs. The other children love working, and I helped my new daughter establish herself in business. When you are advancing in life, and others are not progressing now, they hate on you saying you think you are better than them. I am disappointed that I had to find out later that my in-laws never cared about me. My wife and I went to her sister's house for thirty years with our children to celebrate Christmas and Thanksgiving, and she refused, with her husband, to come to my house because of jealousy. My mother-in-law moved into our house two years ago, and she still has not visited her mother because of me. Her daughter only comes to see her grandmother when she has an appointment for her children. It is sad that family members do not have genuine love.

My mother and grandmother taught me to look out for the elderly. I spent so much time with my grandmother. I read the Bible to her and prayed with her. I took her places and to church. It was a memorable time I could reflect on after her death. Some of my wisest advice came from my grandmother. My mother and grandmother are the most influential people in my life, even though my grandmother passed away twenty-nine years ago. What she taught me stuck throughout my life. She taught me never to be jealous of anyone and to always do good to others. "Do not waste your time trying to hurt someone that hurt you, and you will be blessed. And try to save for a rainy day."

I never thought I would have so many siblings and in-laws against me. I continue to pray that Almighty God keeps me strong. I never expected my oldest brother to resent me when I looked up to him when I was a teenager. Maybe he saw something in me. I was never going to be like him and my father. Maybe he thought I was going to be different from the rest of my siblings. I was different from him and the rest of my siblings. I was always striving to be better. If I made mistakes, I wanted to correct them. After my first marriage was all over, I wanted to better myself as a person. I started reading college books to self-educate myself. I had no idea I was going back to college. After I met my current wife, I registered myself back to college. I read books on how to treat a woman and more about sex. I always stayed to myself. I guessed what was different from them; I never needed to be in their presence. They did not do things I was accustomed to. I did not like gambling and doing drugs and having a lot of girlfriends. My oldest brother always mistreated me in front of our grandmother, but our grandmother told me "not to worry how people treat you and do what is right before God." I took her advice. She said to me, "When he is coming down the ladder, you will be going up the ladder." My brother lost all his four stores because he had a gambling habit. After I lost my own money I gave him to buy a car by gambling with him. I promised never to gamble again with him. He lost all with his bad gambling habit. What my grandmother said was coming to light. He has a high school diploma, and I have a bachelor's degree in management. He has a small house, and I have a multifamily home. I raised my children, and he never raised his children. I have been married for thirty-six years, and he got remarried at sixty-eight years old and still controlling. I have exceeded him in every category in life and is in better health than him. Now I understand what my grandmother told me forty years ago. Now he is looking up to me, that I am a better man than him. And he is still hating today. He never got over his jealousy against me. My enemies are the reasons I am stronger than them. I do not allow jealousy to penetrate my soul. God has given me victory over him. When people meant bad for you, God meant good for you.

My sister is like my oldest brother, possessed with jealousy. She told me I was not going to make it with my wife. Her marriage ended, and me and my wife lasted. Everything I tried, she failed. She tried to go to college but never made it past the first year. She gave up. Her life has been full of misery. I offered her an invitation to my graduation party, but she refused to support me. She said she loves me, but it is fake. My children do not know her as their aunt because of her jealousy. She never visited them, and she lives close by. This is another example of jealous siblings. I never expected my sister to turn out like my brother. It is too bad people allow hate and jealousy to get between a relationship that could have meaning. No matter what wrong my oldest brother did to her, she continued to kiss him. He did all the bad things in life. He never was a good role model as a big brother. He is the biggest loser in the family. It's love being misinterpreted.

I dedicated my life to my wife and children. I promised God I will give them my best. I served God for over thirty-five years as a Sabbath schoolteacher and promised God I would raise them on the Word of God. I made sure the church nurtured them. I never gave up spiritually. At times, it was a struggle having a wife not committed like me. It made it harder for me to focus. But I gathered all of them Sabbath after Sabbath. I wanted to have that family time for worship, but I had to do it alone. I never forced my wife to worship because she did not want to be engaged. But I kept the family together at all costs. It was hard for me, but I continued to cling to God. No matter how I felt at times, it was my duty to feed my children the Word of God. It was not easy for my wife to keep the Sabbath. She was raised on Sunday worship. Although I was raised on Sunday worship, it was not hard for me to keep the Sabbath. In my first marriage, I was converted to Seventh Day Adventists. Once I was rebaptized back into the faith, it was easy for me but not my wife. We struggled the first five years, but I stayed the course. It was the most important decision I made in my life, to return back to God. I do not think our marriage would have lasted if I did not ask God to give me peace. I was heading in the wrong direction. God saved my marriage. I had no grip on it. I struggled for years to stay committed to God. When I joined the church, I wanted to teach the young people the Bible. Teaching kept me grounded in God's Word. I needed so much work in changing my old ways. It helped me to be a better parent and have more understanding. It helped me to keep that love for my wife. It seems so many of my friends are divorced, and church friends' marriages fell apart. I wanted God's divine protection. I am far from being perfect, but I am not where I used to be. I try to be real to my students and people in general. My wife is not perfect, but she always had our six children at heart. My wife has grown spiritually in the last thirty-three years. We are on the same page now regarding the Sabbath. Our life has grown to maturity. We have a better understanding of each other's feelings. We have a lot more things to talk about regarding our children and grandchildren. We still need God's grace in our marriage. Our adult children are still attending church with us. Marriage is something you always have to work on all the time. Life is what you make it. You have to put in the work. No one is perfect. You have to accept the person for who they are, and they have to accept you for who you are as a person. It is easy to bail out when things get rough on you, but it takes love to work it out. Love will solve all your problems with a touch of forgiveness. It is bitter sometimes and sweet most of the time.

Are we always honest in a marriage? In the last thirty-five years, I would say no. Married people are not honest all the time. I know for a fact I have not been honest all the time, and that goes for my wife, but we learned to forgive each other's shortcomings. I cried many nights asking God to help me when I fall short. I encouraged my children to seek God and do their best. "I do not want you to follow me but lean on God for yourself." I am proud of my wife. She came a long way in her Christian journey. We still have some growing to do spiritually. We are not quite there yet, but we are getting there. We are still keeping our children closely knitted. We meet on Thanksgiving and Christmas every year to keep bonded. We celebrate our anniversary and birthdays to stay close.

It is not easy being a father, always worrying about keeping a roof over your family and the necessary bills to be paid. As they grow older, we worry about our daughters and getting pregnant before graduation or finding the right partner or our sons getting a girl pregnant. Fathers that are concerned about their children never stop thinking about them. Fathers are the protectors of the family. Absent fathers open the door for attacks on their children. It is important to take your fatherhood as more important above other things in the world. I knew I wanted to be a great father at the age of thirteen. The negative example my father portrayed was distasteful. He did not protect his family. I wanted to be the one to read them stories or help them with their math. I wanted to be that type of father. I wanted to be the one to discipline them when they did wrong. I wanted to be the one to read them the Bible and pray with them.

There were things I never received from my father. We never had a chance to be raised by him in the same house. I remember as a child my mother took me and my brother to visit him in jail. That was the time he should have been at home to protect us. I was too young to ask my mother why he was jailed. I was about four years old the last time he lived with us after they were divorced. He moved to New York City after the divorce. My mother sent us to stay with him every summer. My mother made sure he stayed in our life. Those summers, his girlfriend watched my brothers and me while he worked. We were well kept by his girlfriend. Betty was always kind to us. She protected us like we were hers. We had some fun times in New York. I remember playing in the street. We were bullied by some Spanish boys, and my older brother had to fight the leader. After that incident, we had no more problems with them. My brother was never afraid of anyone, like my father. My father was short, but he could not be bullied. My father always provided for us financially, but he was not educated to teach us out of any books.

After my mother decided to leave her second husband, we moved to Connecticut. We lived with our grandmother for a short period of time and then moved into our own apartment. I was not happy moving from Virginia, my home, to a new state. I cried many nights, but my grandmother was always there to comfort me. After time passed, I stopped crying and adjusted to my new life. I met some new friends and met a bully. My mother instilled in us not to fight and steal. We were taught to be kind to others, but sometimes people are not kind to you. Bill was a dark-skinned boy, and his mother was also dark. My mother had light skin that could pass for White, and I was brown skinned. Bill always made fun of my mother being White, and I would call his mother Black, so we fought all the time. I hated fighting, but I was forced to fight. I never liked him because he was a bully. The last fight I had with him, I was in the ninth grade. He tried again, and this time, I overpowered him. He never picked another fight. After seeing the abuse my mother experienced from my father, I grew to be against any violence or constant bickering. As a child, witnessing my mother bleed while walking me home when my father hit her in the nose left me mentally paralyzed. My wife and I have been married thirty-six years. I avoid physical contact before my children. What man with integrity wants to walk around the neighborhood with his wife physically bruised up? I love myself too much to see any harm done to my wife and children. I trained my children to talk to the passersby.

When I met my wife, we spent a lot of time together, and I knew she was my soul mate. But I did not know she had a hidden demon to deal with herself. She had moments when she could not control them. She did not know how to deal with complex problems, and she was frustrated at everything. I was not prepared with this type of personality. Most women I dated had control of their emotions. There were times when I did not know to go left or right. This frustrated me in the relationship. I remember one time, she scratched me for no reason, then I realized she could not control her emotions. I tried to question her reaction, but she lacked communication skills and could not explain why she responded physically in an abusive way. I did not take it in a negative way because she was actually attacking me. It was something beyond my control I had no clue what she was actually going through or been through before I met her. I was not accustomed to this type of behavior. This was all new for me. I was not used to any woman putting their hands on me. My mother raised me to be a man and not to hit any woman. The first time I was struck by a woman, I retaliated because I was not expecting that behavior. After I was struck by her, I decided not to strike back. After telling her never to put her hands on me again, she never did it again.

You never know a person until you spend time with them. I could never understand my wife's emotion; she was never open to me. It was so bad the first two years I did not know what to do with her outburst for no reason. Something happened in her life that caused her to withdraw her feelings, and the only way was to lash out at the person she loves. She suffered from low self-esteem. She did not know how to deal with her emotions. She is a good wife, which helped me to understand why she was so angry with herself. She suffered from her father being abusive to her mother, and she was abused in a previous relationship. There was no love in the house. She watched her mother showing lack of love for her father and her father having no respect for her mother and her father uplifting her older sister but downplaying her. All those mixed emotions caused her not to open up in our marriage. The only way to relieve that stress in our marriage was taking it out on me. I began to feel pain myself, so I rebelled against her bad behavior. So I stayed out every weekend partying and hanging out with a female. This was my way of escaping. It was hard to get her to open up to me. I did not know where to go with the marriage. So I escaped through the night life. I knew I was never going to leave her because I really love her. I believed in taking care of my family. I did not have a problem with her physically abusing me because I knew how to restrain myself, not hitting her, and she knew she could not manhandle me physically. So she used words that could hurt me. I often fell into her trap, so I said negative words to fight back. She always caught me at my lowest point when I have worked all day lacking mental judgment.

After two years into the marriage, I figured it out I would have to learn to deal with her behavior. After she got pregnant with our second child, I stopped hanging out in the streets. I gave up the night life. I joined the church and started relying on God on how to deal with my wife's split personality. I had to stop using the night to avoid my problem. I had to learn how to deal with my wife's mixed emotions. It takes hard work and love to keep a family together. You learn to accept someone else's shortcomings as well as your own shortcomings. If most couples understand the dynamic of each person and how they were raised as people, they would have a better understanding to deal with that relationship. My wife came from a totally different background that I was raised in. I grew up without a father in my household, so I did not have to see abuse. I was happy being raised by my mother. She made sure we had the love of God by sending us to church. My wife grew up in a home with two parents living in the same household but with no love. Her father was no better than my father, not living at home. Both fathers did not protect their homes. They did not protect the love that their family needed but gave it to other females not part of the family. They brought their mistresses in their family lives. They did not guard against evil; both men were never filled with God's love. What your children see in their parents will travel into their relationship and when they get married. That is why we married. We must understand the dynamic of each other's family to make our family better. The first five years are when you are getting to know each other as human beings. The most important thing to remember is not to get lost in your own feelings but try to understand your partner's feelings. My wife was not the most open person about her feelings. It took years to bring it out. I realized instead of focusing on my own hurt, I tried to understand some of the pain she experienced before she met me. I spent so much time protecting my own pain from the past and never thought of her pain. So I asked God to help me to heal and help me to correct things I needed to change in me.

As I grew into our marriage, I realized we had the same pain. When she was overlooked by her father, I experienced the same pain being overlooked by my father. I was never treated the same like my brothers, and my wife was never treated the same like her sister. Some people might wonder why my wife was so bitter at me sometimes, but she was not bitter at me. It looked like she was bitter at me, but she was trying to overcome past feelings that had nothing to do with me. I understand my wife better than anyone on the planet. That is why I still love her. I allow her to grow as a person. I am the strongest out of both vessels, so it's my job to continue protecting her in a positive way. My wife and I have the same goals: love our children equally and make sure they are loved by both of us. This love is passed down to our grandchildren equally. Love is only everlasting when you put your spouse or significant other as your main attraction. God meant for marriage to be enjoyable, not a nightmare. Sometimes I said negative things to my wife because she said negative things to me, but I was only reacting from pain. When I think about it, my reaction tells me to have more self-control over my feelings. I should be a little more understanding about her negativity. She could be experiencing some type of ill feeling about something that happened that day. And she needed to channel her anger to me, and I failed to comfort her at her low point and reacted negatively when I could have made her better. This is love misinterpreted. So I guarded my hurt feeling by responding negatively. We are humans, not taking the time to think it out. Marriage is hard work. It's a lifetime of love. I have learned to control my pain to avoid more pain. Our marriage began to mature as time passed. In the past, my wife's father stated that if I stayed married to his daughter, I would become a drunk like my sister-in-law's husband. But that did not happen because I never depended on any substance to avoid my problem. But I did turn to illicit sex, but I walked away from it. I had to focus on my wife.

We both gave our life to Jesus, and her personality started to improve over time. I remembered before she was baptized, her emotions were out of control seven days a week for no reason. She was angry with herself. After she was baptized, it narrowed down to one a week. My wife has always been a productive wife. I made a promise to God that if my wife was willing to get baptized, be a good mother to our children, and be productive, I could deal with anything that comes in the relationship. If I had to deal with her uncontrollable temper, I would help her as a person to be better. My wife has worked hard trying to be emotionally supportive to me. I never see my wife ever displaying her emotion to any other person but me. I was her outlet to channel all that past hurt. I understood my wife, so I decided to deal with her mixed emotions. When she verbally tried to hurt me by her words, I learned how to handle her. I did not take it to heart because she was actually angry with herself. I was her outlet to vent those feelings out. When the preacher says for better or worse, most married couples forget about the worst. They are only concerned about the good in the relationship. When do we as couples realize there is the worst in the relationship? My worst was dealing with her emotions, and the good was she is a faithful wife. I love her, so I was willing to deal with the worst. So I accepted the fact that if I restrained my emotion from attacking her emotion, I could help her rid some of those emotions in time. After our third child, she was better at controlling her feelings. But if we do not continue to work on the things that could make our marriage better, we could slip back into our old ways.

After our fourth child, I settled down completely. I asked God to help me work on my imperfection, and he would work on my wife's imperfection. It was much easier for me to deal with my wife's mixed feelings. I took the focus off her and focused on what I could do to make it better. I was growing mentally and spiritually, but I still felt my wife was not trying hard enough to make it better. I felt lonely at times. She was not communicating to me about her feelings. I was so depressed I told her I was leaving her. I was at my lowest point in the marriage. I was not happy after sixteen years. She always made those comments, and she was not happy. I remembered her coming downstairs crying that she would work on the relationship. I could not leave her. The Spirit of God would not let me. We both worked harder on our marriage. If she never came down crying, I would have walked away from the marriage. I realized my wife did love me, and she had to work on her emotions. She did improve on her attitude. In the next five years, things were better. The worst became better. We communicated to each other about our feelings. We continued to communicate with each other. I saw a good wife in her, that's why I married her, but I had to put the work into the relationship to keep her. I always depended on God before I make a wrong decision.

Chapter 7

All our six children are adults now, and we are still keeping it together. Our children play an important part in our life. They are the reason we stay closer each year. We celebrate our birthdays and anniversaries every year. We keep the family united together. We demonstrated to our children that relationships are something you work on daily. You will have those moments you will not always agree with each other, but forgiveness and love work together. We still have our disagreements, but it is nothing to keep us apart. Love is often misinterpreted.

My wife never hated my daughter whom I claimed the first time after she came into my life at twenty-one. I never knew she existed. My wife would not accept her unless DNA was taken. I failed to take the DNA test at that time. I ignored my wife's advice. My wife would not to accept her and her children as family, in which she was right. I made that choice to be her father without taking the test. I got so involved being a father I overlooked what was important to my wife, taking the test. I should have taken the test, but now my daughter refuses to take the test. I do not know for sure if she is my blood based on her mother's character. I met a girl in Norwalk for the first time. She told me she broke up with her boyfriend, and he moved down south. The next week, she came to my house to have sex. I was only eighteen at the time. She called me on the phone asking for money for an abortion. I refused to give her money for an abortion. I did not believe she was pregnant by me. I never heard from the girl anymore. So after twenty-one years, a girl I went to school with said the girl had my baby. I asked her who the girl's mother was. She said

Dee was her name. I said I remember her. So she gave me her daughter's number. I called her mother's boyfriend, and the woman said she moved into her own apartment. I called my daughter's house, and her sister answered the phone. She told her, "It is your real father," and everyone seemed to say I am the father. I met the lady at Caldor department store. I claimed the girl based on her voice. She sounded like a little country. I found out six months later when her mother was let out of jail she was from South Carolina. I got involved too quickly, but my wife wanted me to take a DNA test to make sure she is my daughter. I had already told my children she was their sister. I got her too involved with the children. No matter what I did for my daughter, my wife would not accept her as family. I can't blame my wife, the way she felt. She was right. After twenty-one years have passed, my wife is still not going to accept her as family, and I have to agree with my wife. I do not know if she is blood. But with all the things I have done for her, I am her father. I still love her, but I cannot see me being her father again unless the lie her mother told is straightened out and a DNA test is done. I do not care what I did for her the last twenty-one years. I want to know the truth. My wife is an understanding person, but my daughter made it even harder to accept her as family because she used me all those years for material things. She never wanted that father-daughter relationship. And even if the DNA test will prove she is my daughter, I still could not have a relationship unless the lie told about me was straightened out. She would still blame me for not being there in her younger years because so much hate has been built up. I pray one day she makes the right decision to find out the truth. It makes it harder for my wife to accept her knowing she has not spoken to me in seven years. She has not made any attempt to make it right. My wife is a fair person when it comes to doing the right thing. My wife has been very supportive of our other children. After all the drama, my wife and I are holding it together under all the pressures of life. It is not an easy job keeping everyone connected, but we are making it work. My wife is a peacemaker. She wants the best for us.

I thought after twenty-five years, my daughter would have been healed because my nephew molested her at seven, but she did not heal or forget what happened to her as a child. I knew in the past we discussed it in church about forgiveness and letting God heal her.

So I was giving a birthday party for my wife and me in November. I invited my oldest brother and younger brothers' wives to celebrate our birthday. They lived in Virginia, and because of COVID, I did not want that many people at the party. My next to oldest brother had no idea our nephew did that to my daughter, so he invited him to the party. I did not invite my nephew because I did not want my daughter to be uncomfortable at the party. My family has the tendency to invite the whole family when parties or any picnics are happening. When my daughter heard the news that my nephew was going to be there, she assumed I invited him. She cussed me out on the phone. I had to explain to her I had no idea he was coming to the party. I had nothing to do with it. "It was your uncle who invited him, and he had no idea you were molested by him." So we agreed to deal with it. And we did have the party and had fun listening to the music and dancing. All my daughters prepared the food for that night. We always work together when we give parties; it keeps us united as a family. My children are very supportive, looking after our welfare. The DJ played the music all night, and we enjoyed ourselves. Everyone was content after the party was over. The next morning, we all talked about how we had a good time. My family went back to Virginia.

My daughter never talked to me about my nephew until months later when I decided to have my anniversary party in March. I invited my sister and her boyfriend to celebrate to see if she would come when I invited her. She came last time when my brother invited her. She never came to my house because she had issues with me from thirty years ago. I wanted to see if she did care for me. My sister's son put it on Facebook. I was the black sheep, meaning no one cared about me. He must have gotten that from his mother. I responded back to him that I was never a black sheep. I was different from them. My siblings did drugs, gambled, and other ungodly things which I did not do at all. I was clean-cut. I was strictly a family man. I stayed away from them. I also invited my nephew and his wife back thinking my daughter was over the situation. She told me she would not come if my nephew was coming back. All my daughters convinced me that if my wife's brother was banned from coming to my house because she molested my oldest daughter, it would not be fair for my nephew to come back. I had to make a decision on it. I decided to call my nephew to let him know he could not come to my anniversary party because my daughter never was over the matter that he caused her. It was hard for me because I watched him grow up as a child, but my daughter and children are more important to me. It was important that all of my children and grandchildren were there to celebrate with me and my wife. Once my family heard that my nephew was not coming to the party, my sister and brothers decided not to come to support me. My friend's cousin decided not to come after talking to my sister because she and my sister are best of friends. They did drugs together with my nephew. My friend's cousin also called my nephew to see if he was coming to the party. All these have their clicks. My friend's cousin had the nerve to call him about the party. She wanted to know if we had fun so she could report to the others. He told her we had fun. Family does not always come around you because they love you but because they want to be around others they love. I am saddened that love is not always displayed in the Black family. My sister never cared about my wife and children because she never came over, and I was not her favorite brother. That is why I never believed her when she told me she loved me. Her actions tell me she doesn't care about me. After calculating all the years she never came to my house, I realized she does not mean any good, so I decided not to visit her anymore. I hate one-sided relationships. My wife and I feel the same way about a lopsided relationship. I have no plans to invite my sister to any more functions again. I will not let my oldest brother invite anyone to my house unless they talk to me.

I love being around people that appreciate my kindness. I do not need to believe people around me. I teach my children to be real. Life is not always the way you want it, but you can continue to make life better. My family has always been the most important part of my life. I work hard for them. I try to be the best father and friend I could be. I am serious about life. I value family that value themselves. I stay away from families that have no values. I know my enemies, and I know those who care. Most of the people that do not care for me are the people that are jealous of me and my family. Most of my siblings do not have that close relationship with their children like me. My children always have me and my wife at heart. They show their love and appreciation for us. I am blessed. My mother had a small talk with me when I was eighteen years old. She gave me some important advice: "If you take care of your children, they will take care of you." I made sure I supported all of them the day they were born. We may have our disagreements, but we always fall back in place. We know how to love without hanging onto a grudge. I always tell them God's words of forgiveness. My mother was right about the advice she gave me, and it came back with many blessings. My children are not going around talking behind my back that I did not support them financially, but my brothers' children are talking about them. That is why they consider me the black sheep because I made the right decision when it came to my children, and they did not make the right decision by their offspring. I am happy I am the black sheep if they want to call me that. All their attacks on my life and children made me stronger and better. I am glad I have a God that has been watching over me. All my children are productive citizens. I did something right. I am happy that my mother gave me wise advice about staying away from jealous family members. They could hurt you if you are not careful. I am happy that jealous family members do not want to come to my house. I do not want my children exposed to hate. I will continue keeping my children and grandchildren united in love. I will not allow any outsider to break that bond with my children. Siblings that are jealous are not good for your health. It can cause you to be ill like them. I want a good healthy life. My sisters and oldest brother could never experience joy in their lives because of hate. My nephew, who calls me a black sheep, is the main person who talks about how bad his mother was on Facebook when she works hard to keep a roof over his head and support his oldest children when he fails to support them. This is another sign of jealousy. He is the same nephew who robbed me out of $800.

I never could understand why a grown man would want to molest a child. I could never see myself hurting a child. The people closest to you are your worst enemy. I would never have thought in my wildest dreams my blood nephew would attack my daughter. I could see an outsider doing something like that but not my own family. When my daughter told me, I was not close to him anymore. I admired him at one time, but now I see him as a loser. It was not the same with my brother-in-law that committed the same act; this is someone I observed from a baby to an adult. I never forgot the situation, but I allowed myself to heal inside from those child molesters that brought my daughters' spirits down. I am deeply sorry that my daughters had to change in their life. I saw the pain in both of my daughters' spirits when they were attacked by family members. There were tears running down their faces, emotional from the abuse. These men never tried to apologize to my daughters after years passed. The child molesters are in self-denial about attacking my daughters. It makes it harder for them to forgive them. I continue to pray for my daughters' healing. I cannot imagine what they went through as a child. It took me years to get over those feelings. I thought I was all right, but I realized I was traumatized about the incidents. I pretended I was fine, but I was not fine. They are my blood. These are family members. I had their back. I am still trying to digest why I am so good to my nephew and brother-in-law, mainly my nephew since I watched him grow up. Maybe my nephew was jealous like his father but I did not detect it at the time. I thought he was different from his father—he is just like his father. They do not care who they have sex with, even if it's a dog. I pray for those men that they repent from their sins. My nephew's wife wanted to apologize for my nephew to my daughter, but I told her not to do it. It is his responsibility to apologize for his offensive behavior. If he apologized from the heart, it would be more effective to her. It could not erase the fact that it happened, but it could help with the healing. I thank God I have some strong daughters. I am glad I spent the time mentoring them back to health. I do not know why good things happen to good people, but I know God has the answers. It made me a stronger father and a better listener. I am more careful about leaving my grandchildren with family members. I am blessed that my daughter overcame the attack and finished college, and my other daughter is raising her sons to be decent people. They both have confidence in themselves. My wife had the same emotions as me. She had to heal from the situation as well as me. My wife had to endure the pain and suffering knowing her daughters were molested by family members. My daughters are living healthy lives now. I have no connection with my brother-in-law. I was never close to him since the day I married my wife. My nephew, I do have a connection with him due to the same family members who gather on occasion. I have few words to say to him, but I remain kind to him. I have no hate for him. I cannot trust him anymore. You have to be kind to your enemies and those who despise you. I cannot walk around being mad because it happened many years ago. Life is not fair, but you make the best of it. We cannot predict when bad things are going to happen to us. We just have to be prepared for the worst and let God work it out for us.

I did not know my daughter was going to turn her back on me after I put her on her feet financially. But I understand that she was raised around aunts and uncles that did drugs. My daughter's mother spent years in jail selling drugs. She didn't have much of a mother figure. Her mother was not a good example of a role model. She had no real father in her life. She spent twenty-one years not knowing her real father. Her mother fabricated a lie he did not want her and wanted to abort her. The people she was raised by knew nothing but the street life. They knew how to take advantage of people by lying and stealing. I am surprised she came out a little better than her people.

When I met her for the first time, she seemed to be this innocent young woman, but as time progressed, I saw another side of her. She has been bitter against her biological father since her mother told her that lie. She had two children when I met her and a deadbeat boyfriend. She was going to college and had a job. She beat up a car. I did not find out years later she had those same negative characteristics as her family—being dishonest. I stepped into an unknown world. I got too involved with her financially without taking the DNA test.

I blamed myself for not taking the proper steps. I made my mistake not taking any DNA test, and her mother made a mistake lying on me. She never accepted me as her father from the beginning when I met her. She never wanted that father-and-daughter relationship. It took me twenty-one years later to know what she wants from me. All she wants is to be connected to my name and get money and favors from me. She was raised to use people. I completely understand why she wants me in her life—to use me. I could not see it in the beginning when I first met her. Years later, it came to surface. When I met her, she was polite and decent. That's what it seemed back then. Now since I established her credit, bought her house, and helped her from losing both her businesses, she became arrogant. She started disrespecting me with insulting words. The way she spoke to me was not the way when I met her. She called me rude on the phone when I asked for money when I fixed her day care. She once told me I was no good because I refused to give her a person's name. My daughter's employee was having a conversation with my other daughter about how the workers would go out to lunch to do drugs and come back to watch the children. My daughter's employee had no idea they were sisters. Every time I would disagree with her, she would not speak to me. My wife hated the fact she was using me. She was a nasty person. It took me twenty-one years later to discover her true character. I do not regret doing those things for her because it came from my heart. I was never trying to make up for lost time because I didn't know she existed. If I never met that girl downtown who told me about her, I still would not have known today. But I thank God I helped another person get on their feet financially. When she could not get her way, she referred to me as her so-called father. After all this has happened, I am not sure if she is my biological daughter. She has too many negative traits to be my daughter. I pray one day she makes the right decision to find out if I am her biological father. After our last disagreement six years ago, I am not sure she is my daughter. My wife has those same feelings. Most of my daughters feel she should take the DNA test to clear the air.

I have had many disagreements with the six children I raised, but we always made peace. My six children love me, but this child never had that love. She is full of animosity. I thank God I have worked on my spirit the last six years to heal from this experience. I always bounce back from any situation that is not healthy. I have always been a strong Black man. I survived my last two marriages and am surviving my marriage now. I never read in my Bible life is always going to be easy. But as long as you have God, he will make it easy for you as long as you submit to his will. I tried being a faithful husband, but it is not easy. I tried being the best father I can be, but it is not easy. I work hard trying to be kind to all people, but not all people are always kind to me. It has never been easy supporting a family, but I found a way to make sure my children had the necessary things in life. I taught them God Word which is a priority. I gave them love and unity. They always had a roof over their head, clothes on their backs. They had some form of entertainment. I made time for them and am still making time for them. I taught all my children how to read and write. I took them to the park to play. I took them to the movies. I took them to the doctors and their dentist appointments. I faithfully took them to church. I did the duties that a mother usually does. It was not easy having all the weight on my shoulders, and still today, I carry all the weight on my shoulders. My children appreciate all the small and big things I have done for them.

My wife does not fully appreciate me. She is self-centered and still that way. After thirty-six years, you would think she would put more into this marriage. She says she loves me, but sometimes her actions tell me differently. I have been asking for years to get help on her split personality. One minute she is the nicest person in the world, but at a different moment, she is the meanest person in the world. It is good I understand those different traits, or I would be divorced. It took me the first five years of our marriage. I have to deal with two people in the same body. I am patient enough to deal with these traits. When the preacher says for better or worse, I understood completely. It took me years to figure it out after running from the situation. But I learned to deal with her split personality. She has a good heart, but she has not learned to master her emotions. I know it takes a lot of work dealing with a difficult person. I had my share of unloving people around me, but I maintain a loving spirit. My last three daughters have those same traits as their mother, hard to deal with at times, but I learned to avoid confrontation that could get out of control. My son is very calm like me. He seldom gets angry. I managed to keep the atmosphere moderate.

I learned to walk away from a person that cannot reason. My grandmother said to walk away from anything that is bad for your health. When you constantly argue, it will turn into a physical fight because somebody is going to say the wrong words from their mouth. I have said wrong words, along with my wife. I turn the other cheek and go somewhere peaceful. I am always working on how to be a better husband, father, and friend. I watched my older brothers run away from their problems instead of dealing with them face-to-face. I observed their behavior so I would be better and more alert. Life is not easy, but you have to work on it. I try to stay positive every day and keep a smile on my face. Life does have its moment. Whoever told me life will never have any problems, I say life is full of problems as long as you live. You will solve your problems as life moves forward, and it will move forward within time. I have good friends, and I we discuss some things that can help me solve and understand my problems. We all need enlightenment. At times, no man or woman is an island, just by themselves. We all need honest, decent people we can trust day to day. My three best friends, I can always trust on them giving me an honest answer when I need it.

My mother was right. My children are my prized possessions. There always will be a woman who will come and go, but your children will always be there for you. I work my whole entire life to secure them from any danger. It is hard raising children in a corrupt society. I promised God I would give them my best. I always had problems with the mothers when it came to the children. Both my children's mothers wanted me to take sides, but I stayed natural. I wanted no parts of favoritism. I hated that word. I experienced so much with my siblings and saw it in other families. I wanted no part in choosing between my own children. I wanted to give them the same love. My mother taught me love. My mother always treated my half brothers and sister with love. I never saw any bias in her. She never took out her anger on children. My mother had always been my eyes. All my life, I tried to walk that narrow path for her, the most loving person I ever knew in my life. I never heard any foul language come from her mouth. I remember I used a cuss word from my mouth. She did not waste any time slapping me in the mouth. I tried using foul language the second time, and she washed my mouth with soap. My mother did not play when it came to discipline. After she disciplined me, I never used foul language again. I practice all through my adulthood. I couldn't have asked for a better mother to be in my life. My mother has always been my inspiration. That's why I made more right decisions than bad decisions. I had a mother that worked day and night to make sure I had the necessary things in life. She instilled morals in me. I guess that's why I always scold my wife about using bad language before our children. She was not a conscious person. Sometimes she used foul language to upset me. She only used it when she was angry, not all the time.

I recall one night, I was sleeping, and she woke me up to fight. I was not accustomed to this type of behavior. I was not ready for her outburst. Not thinking clearly, I cut her with a knife on the leg. It was not a big cut; her anger took me by surprise. My mother-in-law had a talk with me about the incident. She asked me not to ever use a knife. I never did it again. God was looking over me. I could have been arrested if she pressed charges. My wife understood she created that argument. I didn't do it on purpose because I was not fully awake from my sleep. She never woke me up again to fight. I gained more control over my temper. Twenty-five years ago, she was outraged, and she wanted to fight. I locked my bedroom door to protect myself and her from making the situation worse. My first response was to call the police on her to bring her temper under control. She left the house before the police came. She came back later after she calmed down. Sometimes we as men need to put ourselves in a woman's shoes. What would a woman do when a man cannot control himself? She would call the police to prevent physical damages to her. There is nothing wrong with a man trying to protect himself from physical damages. I trained myself to be wise and harmless. I learned to avoid being violent toward anyone. I love my wife. I have to protect her even when she is not trying to protect herself. I guessed with the way she was brought up, witnessing violence, all that anger went in her. It is worse on girls when the love is not there between parents. Marriage is not easy, but you have to work out your differences. You have two people coming from different backgrounds that have to be blended. The good must overshadow the bad. I try to overlook my wife's faults and see the good she brings to the marriage. I can say a lot of good things came from marriage. Six beautiful children were raised as decent citizens. There is no cut-and-dried situation to make a marriage work. Each person has to find their own formula to improve the union. I have seen many marriages fall apart because there was no formula. There was no space for forgiveness. We have to forgive to get through the pain. The longer you hold on to pain, the longer the pain stays with you. If you forgive the person that caused the pain, you will free yourself from the pain. But most people do not want to forgive those that transgressed them, so the pain stays with them a lifetime. It does not bother me if my brother and sister do not forgive me. It is important that I forgive them because then I am free as a bird that was once locked up in a cage. Birds are not meant to be locked up, and we are not meant to be locked up because we cannot forgive. I did not allow them or anyone else to lock me up in a cage because I was free when I gave my burden to God. I fought back with courage.

My brother and I were born from the same parents, but he tried to disown me as his brother. He was telling people I was not his brother. It did disturb my consciousness for a short time, but I bounced back. I was not going to allow his hatred to make me hate him. I forgave him like Jesus forgave me. I am free from his burden. God is my help in time of need. God has always been with me even when I lost focus on him. It is because of God that I can withstand the devil's attack against me. My brothers' and sister's attacks cannot hurt me because I know God will help me. God is love, not hate. I am happy they think I am the black sheep. I see all God's blessings on me. I am moving forward with love. My children are taught to forgive and pray for those that see they differently from them. I never look at myself as being an outcast. I saw myself as a blessing from God. My children have beautiful lives because I had a higher standard for them. Are they perfect? No, they are not perfect, but I taught them about God and morals. I would never want them to be like other people but to be themselves. I do not believe in comparing my children with other people's children. I want them to be how I raised them. My mother never compared me with her friends' children. She wanted me to be my best and to be honest. I can only speak for myself, not my siblings. I will continue doing right even though it is hard sometimes.

After thirty-six years of marriage, my wife and I have grown spiritually. We are able to control our tempers compared to when we were younger. We came a long way, but we continue to work on our lives to inspire our children to do better. I pray those who read this book will gain some insight on how to continue improving your lives. No matter how long we are on this earth, there is always something to learn to make us better human beings. It is not our material wealth that makes us happy; it is about the spiritual that enriches us. In my younger days, I wondered if I had more money, would I be happier? My family would be better, but I was so wrong to believe that concept. The less things I gave them and the more morals I gave them, it made them better and less selfish children. I laid a solid foundation for them. I laid out the blueprint for the next generation. I showed them how a father should protect their children at all costs. And it comes with a price to be an outstanding father. It takes hard work and dedication. I am proud of my work as a father, and I am constantly trying to be a better husband, not a great husband. But I could be a great husband depending on my wife and the way she treats the marriage. It takes two people to be equally yoked; if not, there will be an off balance.

My best friend has been unequally yoked with his wife for years. After high school, he went to the army, and I got married. Years later, he came back home. I was divorced, and he was separated from his wife. He always talked to me about getting his family back together again. I was married now to my third wife. I always look after my friend like a brother. We offered him to stay at our home to get himself together. He stayed probably six months. He had a job. He worked hard like me. He moved out of my house and went back to

Stamford. I saw him on occasion, and we talked about our families. He wanted to get his family back together. I prayed about it that it would happen one day. After me and my wife had our fourth child, I saw him again in Bridgeport, Connecticut. He was back with his family. I was happy for him. God did answer his prayers. After his sons were grown, he made a decision to raise his granddaughters. He raised his daughters' children until they were able to go back to their mother. After his granddaughters moved back down south, his wife separated from him again. His wife and his oldest son rented their own apartment and left my friend with a room. He continued to give his wife money to help pay her rent. The other day, he wished things would have worked out better for his wife and family. I explained to him that it is not who starts the race but the person who crosses the finish line. I opened his mind to not be so hard on himself. "You started out rough, but you ended up well. Your family came back to you, and you raised your granddaughters, so you finished the race." God gave him an opportunity to make a difference in somebody else's life. His granddaughters benefited from him. He instilled God in them. They are living a good life because of him. He now does not feel bad about himself because he understands that he finished the race. He gained a better relationship with his children and grand-children. God did give him a second chance to be a great father and grandfather. My friend always was considerate of other people. Now he can live his life with dignity and respect. I am proud of my friend and his accomplishments. He came a long way. He is still bonding with his son. We are connected more now than before he went to the army. Every year, he celebrates my birthday and anniversary with my family. I can always depend on him when I need a favor, and he can depend on me when he needs a favor.

My other best friend has never been married. He loves dating young girls. But he has problems with them. They want a good time and free benefits from him. The dates never matured. He is in the mental health field. He also came to Connecticut to celebrate my birthday and anniversary. He is not looking for a wife. He wants to be a playboy at sixty. He has known my oldest children over thir-ty-nine years and my other children when they were in my wife's womb. He is like an uncle to them and a brother to me. He knows my whole history about my family. We talk all the time on the phone when he is not in town. We both are looked upon as the outcasts in our families. We have experienced the same jealousy, but we are surviving. We are strong. We are unbreakable. We stand tall no matter the situation.

You do not have to be blood to be family. These two men are my brothers. I love them like my biological brothers. They have imparted wisdom to me like I imparted wisdom to them. We grew together in time. I am happy I have good friends. My wife and my children love these guys.

Now we were preparing for a wedding. This would be the first wedding of a child of mine I would be attending. My two daughters were married but never had a big wedding. My son found a good wife. I love my future daughter-in-law. She would make a good wife and daughter-in-law. I am happy to have her as part of the family, and the rest of the family love her also. My wife was excited that our son was getting married. I am blessed to be part of the celebration. I am proud of my son doing the right thing. I raised him to be a man. He is taking full responsibility as a man. He does have a son by his future wife, and she already has a daughter. They love their children. He is a great father, and I know he will be a good husband. They both work hard to keep a solid relationship. They are very involved in their children's lives.

I am blessed to have six daughters who are very involved in their children's lives. My wife and I are blessed to have our children in our lives. They stand by us all the time. They helped us every year cooking the food and doing the decoration for our birthdays and anniversaries. Home is not a home unless a father is there to protect his wife and children. It is important that fathers pull their weight in the family. My son would not be the man he is today if I was not part of his life. I want him to be a man. I took him to my construction site when he was twelve years old. I made sure he read about construction. I had that father talk about how to treat a woman. I guided his whole life, along with his sisters. He blossomed like a rose. He grew to be his own man. I am happy that I took the time to develop him. I was his role model as a father, not anyone else. I am praying that his marriage be an everlasting marriage like me and my wife. My son is blessed to have six sisters to stand by his side. It is not an easy job being a father. It takes hard work and dedication to be a great father, but I could not have done it without the church family and God being my personal savior. I have worked all my life to keep the family together in unity. It is not easy, but the love I have for my children and grandchildren makes it easy for me. Most people cannot separate their jobs from their family. Your accomplishment on the job does not define who you are as a father; they are two separate entities. People may glorify your work, but it does not define you as a man. Only God can define you as a good father and husband. A man or woman without morals cannot completely define themselves as good people. Fathers must instill character into their children morally. It does not mean they will always make the correct choices, but the foundation is laid out for them to improve as life moves ahead for them. My son made the right choice to take a wife to be holy before God. God created the institution of marriage whether you believe in God or not believe in God. I praise God that he made the right decision. Now his children will follow that path in marriage one day. They will not accept that marriage is old fashioned but, instead, a good way of life for them. They will come to the conclusion it is not God's will to live with a man or woman without being married. It is good for the body and mind.

My wife and I were ready to attend our son and future daughter-in-law's marriage. This is truly a blessing for me because I never had a chance to be at my daughters' wedding. The oldest left town to marry, and the next to oldest was far away and made it simple between the two of them. I am happy they both did get married. I pray my son's marriage will not be like a roller-coaster ride that goes up and goes down. I pray their love be equally shared between them. I never felt my wife's love was equally shared to me. The way she talks down to me does not show me she really loves me. Sometimes I feel it is just for all the material wealth I supply her. I am offended when she calls me out of my name. I hate it when she used the word nigger on me. It is the most degrading word anyone can call me. I hate it when she calls me that word. This is what I meant above love being a roller coaster. It tells me she doesn't value me that much as a man. This type of behavior causes me not to value her that much. I have never been so disgusted by anyone in my whole life. She is the only woman ever to call me out of my name. This is very painful to me. At times I just want to be alone to process that type of woman. After thirty-six years, I would have thought she would have outgrown that behavior. I heard her mother call her father a nigger because she did not have that much respect for him. I never would have imagined she would use that word in our marriage. I have been referred to by other degrading words. When she uses improper grammar, it turns me off. I have to go to a secret place to ask me to not lose faith in the marriage. Sometimes I feel like wanting to be involved with another woman, but I have remained faithful at this point. I always prayed that my children find a person that truly loves them. I am angry with her behavior, but I try not to give up on the marriage even though I feel like not being married. I would say 90 percent of the time I am happy, but the 10 percent I am still struggling with sadness. The things that have been said to me make me feel she regretted marrying me. I am not saying she is a bad wife, but there's not enough love to change her behavior for a better marriage. I do not know if I can last another four years. It is hard for me to walk away based on her behavior. I am grounded on my belief pertaining to God in marriage. It is not easy for me because I love her, but the love is not the same. Maybe it is just my imagination getting the best of me. At times when I show affection, she rebels against it. It is confusing to me. She's the most complicated person I had to deal with in a relationship. I am happy my son's future wife is compassionate. My son is blessed to have a supportive mate as his wife. They are made for each other. It is easy for any man to be forced out of a relationship when his wife lacks compassion. When I talk about the problem in our marriage, she turns it up as long as I am sad, but it only lasts a short period of time. When she wins me back over to her, it is not true repentance but enough to deter me from leaving her. I continue to fall into the trap. I really believe she is not completely happy about this marriage.

But she says to herself she cares about the marriage. I do not know what to believe anymore. I tried everything in the book to make it happen, but it seems it is not working for me. Love is powerful. It is not all that easy to walk away. What makes it hard for me is that I cannot leave her for another woman. God is still watching over me. He is still guarding my heart. I am still trying to stay focused.

My son's wedding was in a few months. I prayed for the best. There is no guarantee you will be happy all the time. God does offer us peace of mind. My son will be all right because he is a very understanding person, and he does not like drama. He is in control of his emotions and very calm when handling problems. I am supportive of him inviting my daughter that has been disconnected from this family for seven years. She was never really connected to this family since the day I met her for the first time twenty-six years ago. I never felt connected to her in my heart, but I tried to be connected. But it did not work out for me. I do not know if we'll ever be connected unless we have a father-daughter discussion. There is too much bad blood between us both, and I do not see myself reaching out to her again. I tried too many times. I gave up on it. I prayed to God for some understanding. Maybe if she decides to attend the wedding, it could be a new beginning for everyone to mend their differences. I love her, but I cannot see me making the first move. I am tired of being disrespected by her. I am staying clear of misdirected anger. I tried being a father to her for twenty-six years. She reminds me of my wife who is bitter and hard to deal with as a person. I am tired of going on roller-coaster rides with sick people. I gave them a hundred percent of me. I need to be thankful to people that love and appreciate me as a husband and father. I can get that love from my son and other five daughters. I get that respect from them. My children that uphold me to the utmost and respect me are the reasons I am holding this family together. I am being recharged by them. This is the main reason I have not walked away from this marriage. One of the reasons I am holding it together is so much love from my children and grandchildren. I have been broken so many times in this life, but I managed to pick up the pieces to keep living. I refused to let my spirit die. I am a fighter and a firm believer in keeping the family together at all costs.

It was getting closer each day to my son's wedding. This would be the first wedding as a father that I would be attending because my oldest daughter was out of town when they were married. The other daughter was mad at me why I did not attend her wedding, but it was all good. Whatever they decide to do with their lives is no problem as long as they are happy. I am very open-minded about life. My son, always a man, is not easily persuaded to do anything against his will. He became a decision maker at thirteen. He always knew what he wanted out of life. I always directed his path. I remember when he decided to work for the competition. It was not a problem to me if he decided not to work in my business. I was happy to know he was working. He always bought his school clothes every year. He reminds me of myself. I bought my school clothes every year in high school. I always had that man talk how to treat his girlfriend and about sex. I prepared him to be a man and, one day, to be a family man. He spends quality time with his daughter and son. He is a great father and will be a great husband. He has that loving spirit. I molded him not to be afraid to take a risk in life. It pays off if you take your time. He turned out to be a gentleman. His six sisters love him. He carried his own weight in life, never looking for a handout. I am happy that he and his mother have a great relationship, but he is no mama's boy. His future wife made it clear to him. "You will not be going to your mother's house to eat her cooking but what I cook for you." My future daughter-in-law is firm with him.

No matter what I or my wife feel about him inviting his sister to his wedding, it was not going to deter him from inviting her. He knew we were not getting along with her. We do not care whom he would invite to his wedding; it's his day. We would support and make sure he would be happy. It would be a joyful occasion for us because my family were coming from Virginia.

No one can mend a broken heart but God. He is a great healer. No one can replace his love. I pray all the time for God to mend my broken heart. My heart is broken so much I wonder if God is hearing me. Only a person with a broken heart can understand pain. She broke my heart so many times. I wonder if it can heal. No one can understand the pain of love unless you experience it. My heart is longing to be healed. My heart was broken when my baby brother died. He was the person in the family that could make you laugh. He agitated me to the end. I was angry. When he became very ill, I had a chance to understand why he agitated me so much. He always caused me pain. He told me why he agitated me. He wanted to be like me, but I did not know before why he caused me so much pain. When he died on his birthday, my heart was broken. Only God can mend my broken spirit. I love him. So many times my heart was broken, and I came back.

My first wife broke my heart when she walked out on me. This type of love is painful, but my heart was mended by God. My wife breaks my heart all the time by being disrespectful. It is so much painful when you give it all, but it turns out to be short. Over and over again, God is mending my heart. My daughter broke my heart over and over again. I cannot explain why you give so much of yourself but get a little back in return. God is still mending my heart. Love is painful. Sometimes I want to be coldhearted, but I cannot be cold. Some of my church family broke my heart, but God mended my heart. Sometimes it takes years for God to mend your broken heart. My heart is mended. I have a God that mends your heart when you cry out to him. I am grateful that God still loves me to mend my heart. No one knows the pain of a brokenhearted person but that person. Most people's hearts that are broken for some reason never get mended. They do not ask God continually to heal their broken heart. In life, we do not know when our hearts will be broken. It is not something we plan to happen. In our families, so many hearts are broken and not mended. I pray for those reading this page to ask God to mend your heart from the past. God has used me to help mend other people's hearts in my family and others. I have asked God to remove all pain from my body.

Love is so deep when you love from the heart. We work so hard to make sure love works, but sometimes it does not work out for us. Daughters and fathers crave to love. Spouses crave to love. Friends crave to love. When a heart is broken because of a misunderstanding, pain replaces love. The hurts linger on for years until God intervenes.

God is the only Spirit that can mend a broken heart. My heart has been healed so many times. I am blessed. God does answer prayers but not when we want him to answer it but when *he* wants to answer our prayers. I have seen my brothers and father break so many hearts and see my sisters' hearts broken. Most of them are still suffering from broken hearts. Most of them have not healed. It is the main reason for so much jealousy and pain. They have not asked God to mend their broken hearts. I have witnessed the same broken hearts among my daughters, but I have seen their hearts mended. I am happy my son found true love. It is a pleasure to see him take a wife. I pray their hearts stay together forever. As a father, I prayed for the day he would find a kind and honorable wife.

My advice to married couples is to never take love for granted. Always look out for each other's best interest. Love is hard to find nowadays. Each and every moment of your life, protect each other's hearts. Do not take the small things for granted. Cherish each moment day by day. In my early days, I failed to protect my lover's heart. I took our love for granted, and someone else captured her heart. I took the small things for granted. And one day, another man captured her heart. Her love was lost forever. I never captured that love again. But I learned a valuable lesson: never take love for granted. You should always be on the alert. Guard your relationship with all your heart. Do not let another take her or his love from you. Too many couples take their eyes off each other's love. They begin to take the small things for granted. And before you notice, the love starts to deteriorate. Love is a serious matter. It is hard to mend a broken heart. I have seen so many couples fall out of love because they did not guard each other's hearts. They were so happy in the beginning and drifted apart in time.

Love hurts. Love requires so much work. Love lost is not easy to forget. It takes time. Some people never get over the loss. So they convince themselves never to love again. This is a big mistake because they spend all their lives not trusting anyone again. They live an incomplete life. Love is a beautiful thing. It keeps the heart beating. Love is all powerful. Love is the greatest feeling you can ever experience in your life. If you ever experienced love, you want it all over again. I can't imagine myself not being in love. The greatest feeling is having someone love you with all their heart. The worst feeling is not having someone love you with all their heart. Love is unexplainable at times and complicated also. I pray that all my children find the right love, someone to love them unconditionally. Do not ever stop your love for each other. Always hug and kiss each other every day. Surprise each other with gifts so often to show your appreciation. It is the most painful feeling that your lover doesn't love you but finds love in someone else. Do not take your love for granted. I never gave up on our love for each other. There are times now in my marriage I do not feel complete love because my love is taken for granted. There were times I wanted to be hugged and touched, but I was taken for granted. The biggest problem with society is that most think only women need to be touched and hugged, but men want it also. Society has it all wrong. Men want to be touched and hugged. Do not take each other's love for granted. Men are human. We have lost contact with reality. We all want love in our relationship. Love is so emotional. Love should be treated equally among partners.

After being married thirty-six years, I feel I am not getting enough love and respect. But I am staying focused on love. I am still fighting for love. I am not taking it for granted. Love can be confusing and misunderstood to the person not receiving it. God helped me to understand confused love, love I could not understand at first. Love overcomes all bad feelings. Love has its peaceful moments when you can hold each other. It is good to look back at how you failed in love in the beginning, failed to stay connected with each other's feelings. Sometimes I think I am losing love, and sometimes I am not losing love. When my partner does not give me full love, I feel I am losing it. When she gives me love, I am not losing it. This is when love is taken for granted, not completely full.

All my life, I had to wait for someone's approval. Now I am fighting back. I remember going to elementary school, when it was time to go to the gym to play basketball, I was the last one picked. My teammate threw me the ball, and I double dribbled. They laughed at me. I did not know I was doing something wrong until later on in life. Every time we played any sports in the neighborhood, I was always picked last or not at all. I was never accepted, or no one encouraged me to do better. When I went to high school, I was not interested in playing sports. I focused on academics. I wanted to improve my reading and writing. Most of my friends who played sports were not smart in the books. I continued to be better in school. I graduated with A and B. I was trying to stay on the honor roll. I was on my way to college, but my plans were changed. I impregnated my girlfriend. I decided to get a job and get married. For five years we stayed married, and then separated for infidelity. But we tried to mend the marriage, but it was useless. The last conversation I had with her, I learned I was not educated for her. So I found some college books and started reading them. I was educating myself. I was preparing myself for college. I did not know exactly when I was going back to college. But I knew one day it would happen. It was one of my dreams, to finish college. I was not good enough for her after I helped her finish design school. I always struggle with people accepting me for me. My father never accepted me like my brothers. He wanted me to be like them, but I was different. I wanted a more settled life. They lived a fast life. They love gambling and a lot of girlfriends. I wanted to mature into a man. My sisters share the same attitude as my brothers. I was never accepted by them, but I am a fighter. I always had a problem with people accepting me for being me. After marrying my wife, her family never accepted me. Some of my church family never accepted me. It has bothered me for a long time not being accepted by people. I started accepting myself as time passed. God revealed to me I was a better person. All those people were jealous of me for being better than them. They wanted to be like me, but they did not know how to be like me. I overcame those feelings of being rejected by people who I thought loved me. Those people are the most miserable people I have ever known.

and spending time with each other is just as important in a relationship. Every time you get a chance to hug and kiss, do it. My wife is the most precious person to me. I tried to keep the peace under conditions that may not allow it. It is important to let each other know you love each other, and never take each other's love for granted.

Then you have the mixed lovemaking when you take it nice and slow, then with a little roughness, making sure she feels you. This is similar to lovemaking when she reaches her climax. I wanted to express my way of lovemaking, but out of them all, I love making love to the soul. There is nothing wrong with adults talking about love. We talk about everything else in the world but are afraid to talk about lovemaking. How deep is my love for my wife? My love is very deep for my wife. But our sex life is stronger than ever. Over-the-top sex is when she switches roles but knowing all your body movement. She gets on top, stroking every movement. This is when she gives it all. Sometimes it freaks me out. She does all the work while you relax. She knows what her aim is, reaching the higher grounds, the ultimate climax. Most people do not like to talk about sex, but I let her know my deepest thoughts on love. It is all about her feeling good inside, not about me. I want her to enjoy me in every way. Rough sex is all about me giving it all, hitting all four corners of her body. I want her to feel all of me. Sometimes she wants to give it all to me. Sex is the most powerful thing on her. Sometimes I do not need sex, but I do it anyway to see if my manhood is still there. As you get older, your thoughts play tricks on you. *Do I still have it?* Some men need some type of drugs to help them, but I still can function without those man-made drugs to enhance your sex life. I can function without them. I want to make love the correct way naturally.

Life is not always what it seems to be or what you want it to be. It has its ups and down. It has its special moments. Marriage is the most complicated situation anyone can deal with in one's life. I have been dealing with it for over thirty-six years. When I think it is getting better, it can make a new turn. When you are happy inside, something brings that happiness down. There is always something to deal with at any given moment. But I always find a way to bring my happiness back to par. My moments of sadness can bring happiness. Life can be fulfilling. It can be joyful and peaceful.

I do not know where I would be without my wife. She has her faults, but she is always in my corner for important things. She makes mistakes at times, but she is real. She speaks her mind, and she never holds back. She always has our children's back. But the new daughter that came into our life is not accepted like the other children. She is not convinced she's mine because no DNA was taken at the time, but she holds no hate against her. But she does not oppose my son for accepting her as his sister. I have mixed feelings now because of the things that happened with our relationship. I do not know what to believe about her being my daughter. I still claim her as my daughter, but I am not close to her and never felt close to her, but I did all the right things as a father. I made sure she was treated the same as my other children. I have not spoken to her in seven years now. My son invited her to his wedding. I accepted it, but I have no idea how I am going to react to her being there. She has never been connected to the family. My wife is accepting it because it's my son's wedding. My wife and I hope for the best for our son. We will enjoy the occasion. My son's happiness is the most important matter to us.

This is what I mean when I say life comes with unexpected surprises. My son knew his mother and I have no connection to his sister, but he invited her to his wedding. This is my son's special day. He wants all his sisters there by his side celebrating this special moment in his life. I respect his wishes. Life is not the way we want but the way we have to accept it. My wife and I always agree, are in one accord with our children. We raised all of them to make their own decisions. No matter what decision they make, we support them a hundred percent. We stick together as a family regardless of the outcome. Love is what keeps my family together. We have no time for hate and jealousy. I wanted to ask him to invite his sister, but I did not want to impose my will. I wanted it to be his decision, not mine.

All my life I cared for others and not myself. Now I am concerned about myself. Now I go shopping for myself, something I never did for myself, always thinking about my family's needs and others. I finally woke up and realized I am a human being also. I love my family and church family, but they can take so much of you. I realized true happiness is that you have to take care of yourself. I finally woke up and decided I have to put my family last. I finally had to tell my wife, "You and the children have to take control over your own expenses." Everyone wants me to pay all their bills leaving me dry. I decided it is over for me paying all the bills when everyone is working now. I finally stopped trying to save everyone that does not appreciate me as a father and husband. I was fed up with all the nonappreciation of me. I took charge of my life. I am number one now and no one else. My life begins to improve now. It is not about the physical things but the spiritual things.

I love my family, but they think I owe them for the rest of my life. I have great children and wife, but they take me for granted. They believe I will always be there for them, which is partially true. My wife is my backbone, but she has those negative tendencies. But I am strong enough to fight through all the negativity. I never had a real family because my mother and father divorced when I was a child. My family is my real family because I follow God's blueprint as a model family. My children are far from being perfect because they all made their mistakes when growing up, but they turned out to be responsible adults. I am proud of all of them, which includes the daughter I met when she was twenty-one. We are not perfect, but we have to keep trying to be perfect in God's sight. I never wanted my children to be like anybody else's children. I am proud of the way I raised them. I am blessed by God to be a great father. My biological father was not a role model for me, but he did support me financially through child support. But he was a man who created money. I did emulate that from him. I know how to create a dollar from hard work. He had always been in my life; he just was not the greatest example as a father, but I love him from my heart. That is the love my mother instilled in me. She had always been my greatest role model, leading me to God and Christ. She is my heart. I am happy to have her as a mother. That is why I cherish my own family, the most influential persons in my life along with my mother.

I do not care about how people feel about me, which includes my church brothers and sisters. I used to be concerned about how they felt about me, but God gave me the strength to love me for who I am as a person. I pray and hope the person that reads this book benefits from all the knowledge I am sharing with them about me. This book is about the life I had experienced. I am striving to be the best I can be to my friends and family. I learned to accept me and love me no matter who does not accept me for who I am. I focused on what I can change within me, not changing anyone else. I leave it to God to change people. That is why I never tried to change my wife. I am happy that I raised my children in the love of Christ. God is the reason why I am a great father because I depended on him to direct my path. I am happy that my son invited his long-lost sister to his wedding. She was an outsider that was never connected to this family. Maybe being invited to his wedding might connect her to the rest of the family. My son reminds me of myself, having compassion for others. I am proud of him.

After my first marriage, I wanted to be a Christian, giving my life to Jesus. So I got married again. We both gave our life to Jesus, but I was fully committed, and my wife partially committed. It was hard on me because we were not equally yoked. I gave my heart completely to God, but her heart was not completely into the Gospel. I put all the work into raising our children. I love this woman from the bottom of my heart. As my children continued to grow, God's Word was the most important lesson for them to learn. So I tried gathering the family together every Sabbath to discuss the Bible. This was family worship. Family worship is all about the family. It is about husband and wife gathering their children together to understand the word of God. It was important to me but not my wife. She always found things to do to avoid family worship. She would iron clothes instead of worshiping with me and the children. I stayed frustrated because of her lack of involvement. I wanted so much to be connected to God, but I could not do it alone without her participation in family worship. This is another example of love being misinterpreted. I tried to do it all by myself until all the children became grown. But I never connected to my wife spiritually because of her lack of involvement.

I gave my children all the tools to work with to survive in this world, but I feel I failed spiritually because my wife never connected to me spiritually. I am not strong spiritually like I should be because I am weak in my relationship with God. I love God with all my heart and soul, but I failed him at times. I did all the right things connecting my children to be productive citizens and how to treat others they come in contact with. My main focus in life was to keep them focused on God and make sure life involves hard work. My wife is a good person, but she never took our salvation seriously. I am not saying she does not believe in God because she is knowledgeable about God. I believe it was how she was raised. But I never gave up on her spiritually. I can never judge anyone's heart, only God. I will continually pray for my children and wife to become stronger in Christ. I have weakened a little in my faith, but I am not giving up. I am striving to stay connected to God, my Maker. What I love about my wife is that she is connected to our children, and she tries to put them in the right direction. She does not compromise when it comes to wrong. And she does not give them everything they want; it has to be earned. Life is not perfect, but it can be rewarding. I am passing these values to my grandchildren. I can say that all my grandchildren are respectable. They are my pride and joy. God has brought me a long way compared to my younger days. I am grateful my children are still involved with God. They do go to church with me on occasion. I am truly blessed to have them come to church. I am not perfect. I do make mistakes at times, but I try to correct them for the better. I do miss those days of family worship even though I did it by myself. It was not all void because they all still read their Bibles.

I am going to end this by saying, I need God more than ever. I hope those who read this book gain some insight about love and pain. I hope people realize we all need God more than ever. I cannot live without him. When I feel I am alone by myself with nothing but emptiness, God is there to lift me up. And I have seen many dark days in my lifetime, but he made me feel I am not alone.

It was now getting closer and closer to my son's wedding. My wife and I were very excited about our son's wedding. But there were a few people we did not care about attending my son's wedding. Since it is his wedding, we would be on our best behavior. It happens all the time at weddings, but you learn to deal with situations you have no control, and you deal with the situations you do have control. My son is always trying to make the right decision. I raised him to do what is right, not what he feels. I had negative feelings about him inviting his sister that never had any contact with the rest of the family, but I always had to support anyone making the right decision. I didn't care too much about my wife's sister, but I would be on my best behavior. It was all about my son and future daughter-in-law's happiness. I wanted the best for them.

Everyone was talking about what they would wear at the wedding. My wife bought a nice dress and pair of shoes. She made an appointment to get her hair done. She seldom went to beauty salons. She prefers doing her own hair, but for our son, she would go out of the way to get her hair done professionally. My son wanted me to rent a tux for the wedding, but I bought my own shoes. I wanted to be a little different. It would be fun because my family would be traveling to Connecticut from Virginia. There would be a lot of them. My next-oldest brother loves dressing up. My youngest brother is not flashy, just regular. My sisters-in-law love being flashy. After the wedding, there would be an after-party from 6:00 p.m. to 11:00 p.m. Everyone was invited to the after-party. My family loves to party and have fun.

This would be the first wedding I would attend regarding my children. My oldest daughter had a wedding, but I did not attend because of various reasons, but I did go to my niece's wedding which was on the same day. My oldest daughter that I raised went to Florida to get married with her fiancé. He wanted his father to meet his new wife. My nextoldest daughter got married in Virginia. I was unable to attend. Finally, I could celebrate with one of my children getting married. I finally broke down and cried for my son's happiness. It took me so many weeks to get emotional. I am welling over with joy. God has answered my prayers. I strongly believe in marriage, and that is what I instilled in all of them. Marriage is sacred, and you will reap many benefits. It is not easy but rather requires so much work.

My wife and I have been married for over thirty-six years. We had our ups and down, but we still managed to love each other. I pray my son and his wife will put in the work to stay happy. My wife and children are the main reasons I am grounded. It is important that the older people set a great example for their children. It is all about keeping them focused on Jesus. Marriage is instituted by God. These are the reasons I do not believe in living with a woman unless I am married to her. This is one of the values my mother instilled in me. It is a blessing in God's sight to be married. All my daughters share those values on marriage. I raised them to respect marriage, not to live with a man. I am blessed they are following what I taught them, along with their brother. We were getting closer and closer to his wedding date. June 25, 2022, is his wedding date. I would soon have a new daughter-in-law in the family. Thai is truly a blessing to our family. It is not always easy finding a good mate these days. My son has a winner. We all love her. It is a blessing for their two children to see them get married. God's blessings will be on all of them and future generations. I have three more daughters left to be married, and that will be a long time, but I am praying for them that God will send them the right mates.

God has done so many marvelous things for me. It was God who helped me overcome sadness after both my divorces. I trusted him to give me peace. It was God who helped me to be a better father. It was God who provided for me and my children financially. It was God who breathed the breath of life so I could see all my children grow into adulthood. I submitted my prayers to God when I was young to provide for me and my family and watch my children grow into adulthood. God did all these marvelous things for me. It was God who helped me fight off the enemy. When I was accused in court for something I never did, it was God who won the court battle for me. God is marvelous in all his doing. It was God who kept me positive through all my adversity. It was God who inspired me to never give up on my dreams. It was God who gave me the dream to finish college. It was God who showed me I am not perfect, but I can strive toward perfection. It was God who gave me a productive wife for thirty-six years. It was God who showed me we all do not agree with each other all the time. It is our marvelous God who continue to work through me year after year. It was God who inspired me to go into business. It is God who stood by me through all my failures in life. How great is God's marvelous blessings. He never runs out of his marvelous blessings. It is God who inspired me to write this book on my ups and downs. It is God who gave me seven children to display his marvelous works. It is God who blessed all of them with financial success. It is God who gave me strength to teach all of them his Word that his Word will continue to the next generation. I could never forget God's marvelous works. It is God who gave me the strength to forgive my enemies and to continue to walk with a smile on my face. Victory is always ours when we appreciate the marvelous things God has done for us. It is God who blessed me with my own house and protected me from losing it. How marvelous his works are. It was God's marvelous work that I had a praying grandmother that instilled his marvelous works in my youth. It was God's marvelous work that my mother sent me to church with the neighbors when she could not take me. It is God's marvelous work that I can help others to see his mercy. I am so happy I can sing my own song about God's marvelous work. God is holy and has all the victory in my life. I will continue doing marvelous things for God. It is God who gave me a few friends and family members that are always supportive of me to help me display God's marvelous works throughout the years. I pray that God continues to work marvelous things in my life. I pray that God continues to use my children and grandchildren to display his marvelous works. I thank God for having an understanding mother-in-law that uses her marvelous works through my children to display his mighty works. I thank God for the marvelous things he has done in my only son's life. My son has found a precious diamond for marriage. I am proud of my son that he found someone to love to continue God's marvelous works in holy matrimony. My wife and I appreciate all the marvelous things God has done for us all these years. I am happy I can reflect back now on all the marvelous things God has done for my family. Psalm 98:1 inspired me to write about all the marvelous things God has done for me. I am so grateful

I can read my Bible to add value to my spiritual life. It is marvelous to be inspired by God's holy Word. It is this scripture that reflect on my life all the things God did for me and my family.

How do you deal with a rude person? You pray to God you do not lose control of yourself. My wife is the rudest person I have ever met in my life. I do not know how I put up with her bad behavior. I asked God to give me strength to deal with it. I was watching my favorite show, and she turned the television off. I am a peacemaker and do not have the time to waste my energy fighting back. So I go to my man cave to keep myself in control. Sometimes I feel like cheating on her to let my steam out. Women are not the only people that are abused. If it was not for God wanting me to respect my wedding vows, I would have left her. I guess I love her enough to put up with the garbage. I do not think I could ever love another woman after her. I thank God my man cave is a place I can go to release the pressure. It is so painful to deal with that behavior. I do not think marriage was ever meant for me. Single life is not meant for me either, that is why I am still married. I am still trying to figure it out. My children are another reason I stay grounded in my marriage. I cannot always run away from my problems. My strength comes from God Almighty. He protects me from all harm. I certainly love my wife, but she needs counseling for her behavior.

We had two weeks left for my son's wedding. It looked like all his sisters would be there. My son is like me. He is considerate of other people's feelings. He knew his sister had not spoken to me in seven years. I tried my best to reach out to her, but I gave up. I am glad he invited her. It would bring some harmony to my family, but a lot of work needed to be done. I felt bad my sister was not invited, but she never was connected to us. She had disrespected me for years. And I see no change in her behavior. Instead of her talking to me about coming to the wedding, she went to my oldest daughter. This is what I meant about disrespect. She could have come to me about it, but she had been mistreating me so long she didn't bother to ask me. We did have some connection in my early years, but the relationship deteriorated during the years. I am sorry we do not have closeness anymore. Jealousy destroyed so many relationships in our family. It is a shame. This is the main reason I keep my children connected. I instilled in them to watch over each other's back. Family is the most important part of our life. Without them, we have nothing. We need good friends and honest family members.

I was preparing for my only son's wedding. My son wanted me to rent a tuxedo for the occasion. I bought my own shoes, and the shoes were sharp. Even though my wife is rude, I met her with that type of behavior already. It is nothing new to me, but I can never get used to that type of behavior. Is it a reason to divorce her? I would say no; it is not a sufficient reason. I am blessed to be in control of myself. I rely on God to keep me stable. I am chilling out in my man cave watching music videos. This is where I come to continue writing my books. I get the chance to put my feelings on paper. Maybe someone will gain insight about staying strong in this life. My children will understand why I do certain things and why I do not do certain things. Life has never been easy for me, but I strived toward perfection. I try to continue to improve myself. It has always been important to me to grow and not stay in the same place. That is why I am so proud of my children. They continue to get better. It makes me feel good inside. My work effort is not in vain; I see it in my children. I could never be a great husband, just a good husband, but I am a great father. My son's wedding was two days away now. I was very excited about the upcoming events. My best friend had to cancel out at the last minute because he had no one to cover for him to take care of his patient. He takes care of the young man seven days a week and all day and night. I was sorry he could not make it. I knew he wanted to come to the wedding, but life is not always what you expect. The only thing I did not like about him was that he refused to answer the phone. I would not call him anymore, but he should not have told me at the last minute he was not going to make it. Even though my sister has no connection to my family and I, it was an opportunity for her to take my friend's spot. I called her up to let her know we have an opening for her. She asked me why she was not on the list. I told her I did not plan the wedding. I had nothing to do with it.

I told her, "If you do not want to come, let me know now."
She wanted to know if my brothers were coming to the wedding. I
said, "If they are not coming, that means you are not coming to the
wedding?"

She said, "Yes, I am coming and just wanted to ride with them."

She normally does not come around my family, and when I
invited her, she never came unless my other brothers invited her. We
did not think it was important to invite her since she never came
around, but I invited her anyway because she wanted to be around
the other family. My grandmother taught me to be kind to others
even if they are not kind to you. I am at peace with myself that I
extended kindness to her. My son would have put her on the list if
we had given him permission. If she did not call my oldest daughter
about being invited, I would not have had compassion on her, but
God softened my heart. She is my only sister by my mother and
father. I overcame her bitterness against me. I did not let her bad
behavior affect me. I am strong about not letting other people's bad
feelings get inside of me. At the end of the day, I love me if no one
else loves me. God is always going to love me. I was looking forward to the biggest day of my son's life. He found a good wife. I am
truly blessed to have another daughter. It is a blessing for my grandchildren to witness their parents getting married. I would prepare
myself for the after-party. It is truly a blessing to find a good spouse
to share your life. They are blessed to have parents that have been
married over thirty years. Marriage can work, but you have to put
the time in to make it work. It is not easy, but it can be rewarding.
Communication is the key to a successful marriage—and forgiveness. My wife and I were very excited to watch our only son take a
wife. My son has all my characteristics except one. He was not in a
rush to get married, but I did it quickly. It was all good. June 25,
2022, is the day. I knew all my daughters would look fabulous, along
with my wife. I too would look sharp and handsome. My book will
end with the wedding. It is a shame my daughter-in-law's father was
not coming to the wedding of his only daughter. I would not miss
the opportunity to give my daughters away. This is a chance of your
life you could never get back. I prayed for her father who raised his

daughter. I do not understand what happened to him, but he is a nice guy. I would certainly be there, and no one was getting in my way to be part of this special occasion. My son's mother-in-law is a down-to-earth person, and she would be there to represent her only daughter. She always takes part in every occasion. She is definitely family oriented. Now I there were two days left for the wedding.

Now it's June 25, 2022. The day had arrived. The bride's father refused to attend his own daughter's wedding. As I was driving toward my house, I saw my future daughter-in-law's father walking far away from his home, not dressed. I started to talk to him, but it was not important to converse with him. My youngest daughter wanted me to go to the bank to get three hundred in one dollars for a game at the wedding. I did not know the purpose of it. My wife, her sister, and her husband were at my house. My wife was driving them to the wedding, and I was driving my daughter, grandchildren, and mother-in-law to the wedding. I did not say too much to her sister because she is a backstabber.

When we got to Monroe, Connecticut, where the wedding would take place, the place was fabulous, surrounded with beauty. My son and my daughter-in-law picked the perfect place. We all took beautiful pictures. All my daughters were at the wedding, even the daughter that has not spoken to me in seven years. My daughter and her husband got out of the car the same time I got out of my car. I shook her husband's hand and hugged her. I never hold grudges against anyone, especially family. I was not going to let anything get in the way of my son's wedding. This was his special day. I was very emotional. This was the first wedding I attended involving my children. My three daughters were married, and I never went to their wedding celebration for various reasons. I was so excited to be there as well as everyone else. It was a special day for me and my wife to see our son married. All the guests started arriving to witness this special moment. It was about forty-five minutes before the wedding started. I was asked to join the wedding party, but I did not know I was part of it. My wife was supposed to be part of it, but no one told her. She was left out of the routine. It was extremely hot outside where they exchanged wedding vows. The wedding started. We were walking one at a time to the outdoors. The bride's mother was part of the lineup. The wedding team was finally up there, and the groom came outside doing his steps. He was facing the lady that would perform the wedding ceremony. Now the bride came out with her son to give her away, but the flower man was throwing down the flowers. She looked stunning and fabulous. I have never seen a wedding gown like it. It was special. It looked like the gowns worn on the red carpet. The person who was officiating the wedding started talking. They both had some very special words to say to each other. It was unique the way they did it. They kissed each other and jumped the broom. Then they walked together with the wedding team back inside the building. My son was now a married man.

We all went inside the building, and small tables were set up for eating. The larger tables were set up for the main dish. All the tables were filled up with guests. The guests also looked nice. Then the wedding couple came out to sit at their special table. Three speeches were made, and I was one of the speakers. After the speeches were finished, the groom and bride did the first dance. And my wife and son did the second dance. They danced to Michael Jackson songs and did a great job. Then most of the guests got on the dance floor. My five-year-old grandson was trying to do the robot that he saw his grandmother do with my son. All kinds of pictures were taken by everyone. The photographer did a great job throughout the wedding, and the music did its part. All my daughters and nieces took pictures together. It was the most beautiful wedding I have seen in my life. I am writing this in the memory of my father, "the complicated man" in my life, the man that live a complicated life, the complicated man that lost his beloved mother at three and was denied his father's love, the complicated man raised by his loving grandmother and three wild uncles. Life was not easy for him. The complicated man grew into adulthood. As the complicated man continued his journey in life, he met a beautiful light-skinned woman. They fell in love with each other. It was a match made in heaven. The complicated man married her and had six beautiful children. Life was good, like being in the garden of Eden—peaceful. The complicated man began to fall by the wayside. The complicated man lost focus and went into the world to make other children. He was blinded by the grass being greener on the other side. The complicated man realized he broke his covenant with God, so he left home like the prodigal son. He wandered in the wilderness for many years to find himself. The complicated man heard the voice of God: "Go back home, my beloved son. I forgive you." The complicated man found happiness again among his children. The complicated man loved them no matter the confusion. The complicated man's life was coming to an end. The complicated man looked toward heaven, and God looked at his heart. The complicated man died in peace. We all had a great time. After the wedding, we went to the groom and bride's after-party. Everyone went home to change clothes. We had a party until eleven that night. I am happy my son found a good wife. We posted pictures and videos on social media. My son and his wife went to Mexico to celebrate their love for each other. My main focus was my son's happiness. I was happy all sisters were in agreement at their brother's wedding. They all were happy to celebrate his day. I am happy to be their father. I had some rough moments in my life, but I kept the family together. My struggles made me a great father and a great husband. I owe all of it to God, my savior.

This completes the last chapter of my life—a successful wedding. My son followed my steps to be a peacemaker and to help me keep his sisters connected. All my hard work paid off, keeping my family connected. And to top it off, I gave my wife six beautiful children and success because when I met her, she was not a happy person. I rescued her from all her miseries. I gave her life by taking her out of her parents' miserable home. The least favorite daughter became God's favorite daughter, and he blessed us with six children we can call our own. I fell in love with her and am still in love with her. We have to be careful how we put people down because the first could be the last, and the last could be first. My wife was happy to see our only son find a good wife, something I have been praying for all my life. The wedding turned out to be the most important part of our life. It overrode my graduation party. It was more important than my graduation party. It was the icing on the cake. My heart goes out to the new newlywed couple.

I had a chance to talk to my brother-in-law about his wife's bad behavior at the wedding toward the end and with my brother about my nephew's bad behavior. It affected me because this was a person that I trusted. Years later, I found out that she didn't approve of me marrying her sister. She said that I think that I am better than them, and it offended me because I don't have the same relationship with them anymore. I don't think that I am better than anybody. God has blessed me, allowing me to prosper in life, marriage, business, and family.

About the Author

The author was born in Norfolk, Virginia. He has ten siblings and later moved to Connecticut about the age of eleven. His parents were divorced, and his mother remarried. He graduated from Stamford High School. He married after he graduated. His plan was to go to college for business. He always dreamed of becoming an entrepreneur after graduation. He graduated from Norwalk Technical College with an associate degree in 2003. His goal was to go back to school after he finished raising his children. He started his home improvement business before he started school at Norwalk Technical College. Later, he went to a four-year college. He attended Sacred Heart University part time in 2012. He graduated from Sacred Heart in 2019. He started a nonprofit organization to help young men. He taught Sabbath school for the youth at Seventh Day Adventist Church for thirty years. He enjoys reading and roller skating in his spare time.

Printed in the USA
CPSIA information can be obtained
at www.ICGtesting.com
LVHW051637280723
753515LV00001B/70

9 798887 513416